"This memoir is an extraordinary tale of inspiration, beauty, and illumination, thoughtfully written with the clarity borne of introspection, insight, and wisdom. We are all the better for it, and I am very grateful to Dan for having shared his journey, his stories, and his revelatory lessons."
— **MICHAEL BERNARD BECKWITH**, spiritual director of Agape International Spiritual Center and author of *Spiritual Liberation*

"*Peaceful Heart, Warrior Spirit* finally reveals all the secrets of Dan Millman's journey, as well as our old friend Socrates. Joy's insights, never before shared in any Peaceful Warrior book, add a certain magic. Dan's story — its authenticity and honesty — left me with a sense of peace and optimism. Dan and Joy are very special people, and this is a special book."
— **JOANNE REID RODRIGUES**, author of *Slim, Happy & Free*

"Here is a man who has devoted his life to mastery, first in sports and then in everyday life. In *Peaceful Heart, Warrior Spirit*, Dan Millman establishes himself as a lifelong student and longtime teacher who has practiced, and perhaps even mastered, 'the Zen of ordinariness.'"
— **ROGER WALSH**, MD, PhD, author of *Essential Spirituality: The 7 Central Practices to Awaken Heart and Mind* and professor of psychiatry, UC Irvine Medical School

"In this true story of a lifelong quest for meaning, Dan Millman is propelled from childhood challenges to practical wisdom. As he evolves from a young athlete into a spiritual teacher, he trains with four master teachers. Dan's four mentors speak to us all. The insights, hurdles, and highlights he shares can guide fellow explorers on their own paths."

— DON MIGUEL RUIZ, author of *The Four Agreements*

"Since 1984, when his publisher proclaimed *Way of the Peaceful Warrior* as 'a book that changes lives,' Dan Millman has continued to do just that. For forty years his books and teachings have been a guiding light to millions of people who've found a peaceful warrior's way of living wisely and well. This memoir reveals Dan's roller-coaster journey to a life founded on wisdom. One might even say that he has become Socrates."

— SANDIE SEDGBEER, author, TV and radio host, and founder of the No BS Spiritual Book Club

"What a breathtaking adventure Dan Millman's life has been! I've devoured his writings since the mid-1980s, and his new book has taken me on a beautiful journey of discovery about the real Socrates and peaceful warrior."

— BRAD WALDRON, award-winning speaker and author of *Present Naked!: How to Deliver Your Presentation with Substance, Style and Sizzle!*

PEACEFUL HEART, WARRIOR SPIRIT

PEACEFUL HEART, WARRIOR SPIRIT

THE TRUE STORY OF MY SPIRITUAL QUEST

DAN MILLMAN

New World Library
Novato, California

New World Library
14 Pamaron Way
Novato, California 94949

Text design by Tona Pearce Myers

Library of Congress Cataloging-in-Publication data is available.

First printing, January 2022
ISBN 978-1-60868-790-9

Printed in Canada on 100% postconsumer-waste recycled paper

New World Library is proud to be a Gold Certified Environmentally Responsible Publisher. Publisher certification awarded by Green Press Initiative.

10   9   8   7   6   5   4   3   2   1

Dedicated to
my personal family,
extended family,
and spiritual family.
May this trail of bread crumbs
help you find your own way.

*May the stars guide you
through the dark and speckled forest,
along winding, passionate paths.
May you learn from your wandering…
so you return both stronger and wiser,
here and now where you make your home.*

AGNIESZKA RAJCZAK

Contents

Part Three: Teaching and Learning in the New Millennium 195

Preface

An Unexpected Life

Not all those who wander are lost.

J. R. R. Tolkien

I want to tell you a true story. A long time ago, I set out on a quest for meaning in the modern world. In the years that followed, I evolved from a youthful athlete to an elder teacher of practical (some say spiritual) life skills. The events and experiences unfolded as I describe them — not metaphorically or in a parallel dimension but in the stormy arena of daily life.

For decades now, in my books and presentations, I've described an approach to living with a peaceful heart and a warrior's spirit. This open path, accessible to anyone, evolved from decades of training in gymnastics and martial arts, and with guides I met along the way. Insight emerged only after lengthy periods of preparation, course corrections, and humbling wake-up calls.

While many authors and role models have inspired me, four mentors had the greatest impact on my life and work. I'll identify them by name in Part Two, but here I refer to them by the archetypal roles they played in our encounters:

The Professor: A Bolivian scientist-mystic who created a school whose curriculum contained a global heritage of spiritual practices progressively leading to enlightenment.

The Guru: An American-born spiritual master whose radical teachings transcended existing techniques, but whose later behaviors left lessons of a different kind.

The Warrior-Priest: A martial artist, metaphysician, healer, and charismatic spiritual rascal who rescued souls and opened doors to my future career and calling.

The Sage: A devotee of reality whose paradoxical teaching — simple yet difficult, practical yet idealistic — brought a new clarity rooted in present action.

My first two mentors, the Professor and the Guru, would inspire me to write *Way of the Peaceful Warrior*, while the Warrior-Priest and the Sage would influence all that followed. Each of them had their gifts and blind spots. They appeared within a vast field of other teachers, gurus, and spiritual authorities, some benign, others dangerous or deluded. It wasn't always easy to discern one type from the other. The circumstance that attracted me to each mentor, and why I eventually moved on, provide the substance of my story.

Some readers may ask: What about your teacher Socrates? Is he one of the four mentors? If not, why isn't he included? An understandable question, since my first book in the Peaceful Warrior Saga blends autobiography and fiction, leaving just enough ambiguity to lend an air of mystery about the old service station sage I called Socrates.

To resolve such ambiguity, I now offer this small revelation: *I am Socrates*. That is to say, the literary character I named after the ancient Greek is a projection of my own psyche. I was not Soc's student but his creator. As my muse, he assisted in his own creation. Our dialogues were not remembered conversations but flowed forth as I wrote them. My 2006 novel, *The Journeys of Socrates*, conveys an imagined life of this literary character and the experiences that tempered his spirit.

To put it another way, *Socrates is real; Dan Millman is a fictional character.* Those of my readers and seminar attendees who desired a teacher like Socrates had him all along. Just as young Arthur had Merlin, Frodo had Gandalf, Luke Skywalker had Yoda, Daniel-san had Mr. Miyagi, and Carlos Castaneda had Don Juan Matus — mentors and students from life and legend — I had my Socrates. His teachings emerged from the experiences I'll describe in the chapters that follow.

Even the most meticulous memoirist is an unreliable narrator, recalling the patchwork of the past through personal filters and biases. As the protagonist of my own life, it would be easy to paint a self-portrait in colors made more rosy, witty, or significant with the passing of time. Still, I've related events as accurately as I can, checking my memories with those of friends and family. I hope authenticity and candor have compensated for any shortcomings. This, the story of a transformative quest, had to wait until now.

Now has always been my favorite time. And while the story is mine, the way belongs to all of us.

DAN MILLMAN, AUTUMN 2021

Key Terms

Spiritual
That which inspires, uplifts.

Some, like me,
are just beginning to guess at
the powerful religion of ordinary life —
a spirituality of freshly mopped floors,
stacked dishes, and clothes blowing on the line.

Adair Lara

Wisdom
Perspective. Realism. Understanding.

Knowledge speaks but wisdom listens.

Jimi Hendrix

Enlightenment, Illumination
Awakening to reality. A realization. A practice.

Enlightenment consists not merely in
the seeing of luminous shapes and visions,
but in making the darkness visible.
The latter procedure, however, is more difficult
and therefore unpopular.

Carl Jung

God
All that exists.

Wherever you turn is God's face.

Muhammad

Part One

FOUNDATIONS

We do not remember days.
We remember moments.

CESARE PAVESE

Experience may be the best teacher, but when do formative experiences begin — at birth, at conception, or, as some sages claim, in previous lives? Whatever the answer, we can agree that our adult selves grow out of the seeds of our childhood.

My own childhood moments provided a foundation for all that followed. I've found it an intriguing exercise to revisit events from my youth, both unexpected and somehow inevitable. My life and career as a teacher and author make sense only in retrospect.

In Part One I lay all my cards on the table — the hands I was dealt and how it all played out. I hope my readers enjoy the game as it unfolds.

Chapter 1

Defining Moments

There are times when your only available
mode of transportation
is a leap of faith.

MARGARET SHEPHERD

E arly spring 1964. 10:15 a.m. GMT.
I soared high above a trampoline, somersaulting through
the air of the Royal Albert Hall, London, at the first World Trampoline Championship. In this, my final performance, after completing two twisting-double flips of a ten-bounce routine, I drew
a complete blank. I had no idea what move to do next.

This wasn't entirely surprising, given that I'd flown in from
California early that same morning. Four hours of restless sleep
lent a dreamlike quality to this frozen moment. And why not
dream? It was 2:15 a.m. back home.

A few hours earlier I'd entered the competition floor to see the
controlled chaos of athletes from fourteen countries on the floor
below, warming up on four trampolines. I saw Gary Erwin, reign-
ing National Collegiate Athletic Association (NCAA) champion

with a diver's form and style, whom I'd previously watched on television. Then Wayne Miller caught my attention, performing a move I'd never accomplished, aptly named the Miller. I was the current US Gymnastics Federation (USGF) national champion, which is why I'd been invited.

Gary, Wayne, and their coaches (who, I learned, would serve on the judging panel) had arrived several days earlier to get acclimated. I was eighteen years old, jet lagged, and alone.

After seeing me do a few basic warm-up sequences, no one would have bet on me. I'd have to rely on faith rather than confidence. *It doesn't matter who wins the warm-ups*, I reminded myself.

Only when I mounted the trampoline to begin my final routine did I realize that I wasn't entirely alone. Scanning the expectant audience, now silent, and the panel of judges, I glanced up toward the announcer's table and saw not only George Nissen, trampoline inventor and host of these championships, but also, to my shock and delight, Xavier Leonard, my middle-school homeroom teacher and first trampoline instructor, beaming down at me.

A thrill rose up my spine.

Now in midair, with everything on the line, I had to keep going, do something, anything — so I did. My body, and years of training, decided for me: One move followed another. Zen bouncing, no mind (*mushin*), as the samurai warriors called it. Others refer to this state of absorption as the zone, or flow, or peak experience.

Many sports and games like tennis, golf, baseball, and swimming require athletic ability, but no one is likely to die during practice. In warrior sports like trampoline and gymnastics, free solo climbing, big wave surfing, BASE jumping, and other extreme challenges, the body is on the line — a moment of inattention, a single slip, can lead to catastrophe.

Years before, a trampoline friend and I would play a risky

challenge game in which I'd do one back somersault after another, until my friend called out a difficult move, such as double-
twisting double back — a shouted command that seemed to
bypass my conscious mind and go straight to the body, which
would then perform the move of its own accord. It felt scary and
exhilarating playing on the edge. I never dreamed that this lighthearted play could mean so much until those moments in the air.

No past, no future, no self. Only kinesthetic awareness as my
body completed one move after the next: a full-twisting double
somersault, another multiple twist...

Uncertain of how many moves I'd completed, I had to trust
my years of subliminal counting, finishing with a one and three-
quarter back somersault, then a double back somersault from my
belly, then landing on my feet. It was done. I looked around, taking in the audience as the applause grew.

Walking back to my chair, I glanced up to see Mr. Leonard
smiling down at me. I felt hands touch my shoulder, clap my back.
The reality finally penetrated: I'd just won the first World Trampoline Championship. I vaguely recall shaking hands with Gary and
Wayne as I mounted the victory stand. The trumpets played, and
George Nissen handed me a silver cup. Bulbs flashed. Cameras
clicked.

As my taxi headed back to Heathrow for the flight home, it
struck me that the driver knew nothing about the competition,
nor did the throngs of Londoners and tourists rushing through
their own lives. That day was only a minor footnote in sports history. Still, my sense of life's possibilities had changed. No, I wasn't a
legend in my own mind (nor would I ever be), but I'd accomplished something real in the first eighteen years of my life that
no one could ever take away.

With a sigh, I settled into my airplane seat as the jet accelerated and I was lifted, once again, into the sky. Unable to sleep, I

drifted down a river of memories about all that had brought me to this place and time...

Beginnings

I grew into toddlerhood in a Los Angeles rental apartment on Silver Lake Boulevard, a busy thoroughfare that was, according to family lore, nearly the site of my demise when I waddled out into swiftly moving traffic to fetch a bouncing ball. My father, who had momentarily glanced to the side, allowing for my getaway, snatched me back from the brink and gave me the only spanking of my childhood.

In another example of early risk-taking, during a family beach outing I made a dash for the rolling waves. Knocked down, I tumbled underwater, glimpsing a rippled blue sky, then sunlit shells sparkling on the sandy bottom before my dad's strong arms lifted me, sputtering, from the surf.

When I was six, we moved into our own home in a neighborhood with an abundance of Japanese and Hispanic families, whose children became my schoolmates. I spent playtime following Steve Yusa, streetwise at nine years old, my sister DeDe's age. Whatever I learned from Steve, I passed on to my younger neighborhood friends, Timmy and Tootie — practicing the dual roles of student and teacher.

One afternoon I tagged along with Steve and his older friends as they explored a house under construction. On that particular day, we climbed our urban mountain to enjoy a lofty view from the plywood rooftop. Twenty feet below lay a big sandpile — instant adventure.

Steve was the first to jump, followed by his friends. "Your turn, Danny," he called up to me.

I approached the edge, then stepped back, my heart pounding.

"Do it!" Steve yelled.

"I can't, it's too high!"

"Come *on!*" he countered. Then Steve said something I'd remember for the rest of my life: "*Stop thinking about it and jump!*"

So I jumped. That moment of courage earned me a few weightless seconds of flight followed by a soft landing, as I sank up to my knees in the sandpile. We spent the next hour climbing up and then leaping off the rooftop. After that I acquired a taste for daredevil stunts, playing on the edge of fear.

Soon enough, I came back down to earth: Enrolled early in kindergarten, I'd forever after be the youngest kid in my classes — socially less mature, physically smaller, slower to grasp math concepts, and oblivious to secrets my peers seemed to understand. Feeling like Clark Kent, I dreamed of becoming a superhero.

Maybe that's why Peter Pan and Superman stood out so clearly during my childhood. In retrospect, Peter must have embodied eternal boyhood and freedom, while Superman represented power and human potential. And both could fly. In search of altitude, I climbed trees, swung on ropes, and leaped off low rooftops with makeshift parachutes, yearning to rise above the everyday world.

Back then, my world was small, my horizons limited. My mother, who influenced my early views, spoke of the Tooth Fairy, Easter Bunny, Santa Claus, and God as equivalent fictions. I felt my father's influence mostly in the arena of health and fitness. Feeling a duty to teach me about my Jewish heritage, Dad encouraged me to try Hebrew School, but it didn't suit me. Without a connection to religious teachings or tradition, I had to find my own way, expressed through a growing, ever-changing faith in the mysterious workings of the natural world.

Boomerangs and a BB Gun

In the 1950s I wandered through a realm of fantasy and episodic memories: Cousin Davy and I, mesmerized by the magician-clerks at Hollywood Magic, traded our allowances for a finger guillotine or deck of disappearing cards. We also threw boomerangs in the park, and I developed enough skill with a bullwhip to snap a straw out of Davy's mouth. I also gained childhood expertise doing yo-yo stunts, shooting a slingshot, tossing Frisbees, swinging on Tarzan rope vines, twirling a lariat, and lassoing everyone in reach. After a stint building and flying a box kite, I took fencing lessons before diving into ventriloquism with my own Charlie McCarthy hand puppet.

Practicing all these skills taught me early on that everything is difficult until it becomes easy.

After many entreaties, my dad bought me a BB gun, which came with a lecture on its safe use. I was a good shot and practiced with the same obsessive passion I'd devoted to my former pursuits. But one day, on a whim, I took aim at the tiny shape of a bird sitting on a wire three houses away, never expecting to hit it. I took the shot, then saw the bird fall. Worried that I'd wounded the bird and it might be suffering, I ran down the street, climbed the stairs, and clambered up onto the roof. The bird lay dead with a BB hole in its head.

A few weeks after that, as a sparrow flew overhead, I casually whipped the gun barrel skyward and, without even aiming, took a wild shot. In the next instant, the bird plummeted into some bushes. Horrified, I ran to search for it. As I approached the bush, the sparrow took off and flew away, much to my relief.

That same day I gave away the BB gun.

Tutus, Tights, and a Trampoline

When I was ten years old, two seemingly unrelated events pointed toward my future.

Because my mom, who played piano for a modern dance class, didn't want to pay a babysitter, I found myself surrounded by leotards and tutus in a class comprised of about ten girls and me, all of us in tights at our teacher's insistence. Despite my initial reluctance, modern dance taught me muscular control, suppleness, rhythm, and how to point my toes.

That summer at a day camp, I chanced upon an old ground-level trampoline that liberated me from gravity, if only for a few seconds. After that, I spent every spare moment bouncing, mostly alone, trying to figure out a forward somersault. During my final week, I tried repeatedly to make it all the way around to my feet until I flipped so fast that I landed on my face, scraping it badly enough to raise scabs on my forehead, cheeks, chin, and upper lip. But my toes were pointed and my enthusiasm undiminished.

A year would pass before I found another trampoline.

Bullies

As a child I favored books like *The Story of Ferdinand*, about a bull who preferred sitting quietly and smelling the flowers to battling in the ring. Smaller and younger than my classmates, and at times too talkative for my own good, I attracted the attention of an angry boy who punched me. More surprised than hurt, I avoided him after that.

A second incident occurred in the sixth grade. Another boy took a dislike to me for reasons I don't think either of us understood. He somehow influenced my classmates to stop talking to me. I dreaded going to school for the next few days. My stomach hurt, and I lost my appetite. Then the bully and a few of his friends caught up with me on my way home from school. After making some threats, one of them punched me in the stomach. Satisfied by my tears, they walked away. After a few more days of being shunned by everyone but my two best friends (who spoke to me only in whispers), I felt desperate enough to ask my teacher if I could say something in front of the class. Puzzled, she said okay and quieted everyone. My voice quavering, I told the other kids that it bothered me that no one would talk to me. After that, everything returned to normal, but it made me begin to ponder why people behaved the way they did.

That summer, carrying my lariat, I led my younger protégés, Tootie and Timmy, to the Silver Lake Playground. As I was showing them how to throw the lariat, three bullies surrounded us and threatened me, demanding the lariat. With lips trembling and knees shaking, I handed it over. They used it to tie me to a telephone pole just outside the playground. Then, laughing, they departed, leaving Timmy and Tootie to untie me. My cheeks still wet, I walked home with my head down, my young friends following silently behind me.

The Warrior's Call

Finally, my childhood fear and sorrow boiled over into anger. Tired of feeling intimidated, I asked my dad how I could learn to defend myself. He took me to a boxing gym, but I didn't like getting hit or hitting someone else, so he arranged for a few private lessons with Bruce Tegner, a Hollywood karate sensei to George Reeves, who played Superman on TV. Sensei Bruce taught me a few moves that boosted my confidence. Best of all, he gave me an autographed photo of Superman.

By the time I was eleven, my body was going through changes, and so was my neighborhood. An empty lot up the street, once a forest of palm trees, was now a new Japanese cultural center. On opening day, Dad and I watched a judo exhibition in which children threw larger adults to the mat using leverage. Each of the attackers landed with a thudding slap, breaking their falls without injury. A week later I started group classes two nights a week in a *dojo* (school of the way) with many Japanese students. I liked the bowing rituals and traditions as well as my *gi*, or uniform, tied with a brand-new white belt.

Over the passing months I learned judo rolls, breakfalls, and throws. A friendly, red-haired giant with a black belt named Gene LeBell let us kids throw him to the mat, which delighted everyone. At my first tournament, matched with a boy my age who outweighed me by twenty pounds, I tried a circle throw (*tomoe nage*). He fell on top of me and pinned me. Judo practice soon gave way to other interests, like acrobatics, where my success didn't depend on someone else's failure.

Chapter 2

Rebirth

Teachers affect eternity;
they can never tell
where their influence stops.

HENRY ADAMS

As the saying goes, "The two most important days in your life are the day you're born and the day you learn why." On my first morning at middle school I was about to discover an important why: My homeroom teacher Xavier Leonard, a former acrobat, announced that he was starting an after-school trampoline and tumbling club. "Who might be interested in joining?" My hand shot up.

That club and acrobatics became the anchor point of my day, the center of my life. I practiced trampoline skills in my imagination outside of class, and did endless handstands in our living room, falling repeatedly onto a few throw pillows on the hardwood floor. I soon learned cartwheels, stable handstands, and handsprings as well as basic skills on the trampoline.

By the end of my first semester, I was the only one in the club who could stand atop Mr. Leonard's shoulders, then jump off, land on the trampoline, and do a somersault back up to his shoulders.

One afternoon, after the other kids had left, a smiling man entered the gym. Mr. Leonard introduced his old friend, George Nissen, inventor of the trampoline on which I was bouncing. Mr. Nissen asked me to show him a few moves. Self-conscious but eager to please, I did some basic flips, acutely aware of their imperfections. Then I performed a difficult move I'd just learned. It was called a Cody — a backward somersault from a belly land-ing. Seeing me struggle, Mr. Nissen hopped up and demonstrated a three-quarter backward somersault, landing on his belly, say-ing, "After this lead-in move, Danny, you'll find it easier to do the Cody. Why don't you try it?"

I declined, muttering, "I'll … maybe tomorrow." (Usually game for anything, I was afraid of messing up and looking foolish in front of Mr. Nissen.) He shrugged it off and spoke to Mr. Leonard about other things.

I walked home that evening under a dark cloud.

Seven years later, I would see George Nissen again, at the Royal Albert Hall in London.

Through Adversity, Strength

The bullies were worse in middle school. In the hallway between school periods, a boy I didn't even know walked up to me, wrin-kled his face in a sneer, and called me a "dirty Jew." Then he turned and walked away. It was the first time I'd ever heard the words *dirty* and *Jew* used together. Since I showered regularly, I was puz-zled by his words and shaken by his tone of voice.

Soon after, another tough guy confronted me outside the gym. Despite my attempt to avoid eye contact, he grabbed me in a headlock and threatened to punch me as a crowd of onlookers gathered.

I was bent forward, frozen in his tight grip. All the judo moves I'd learned flew out of my head until I remembered a simple move my dad had once shown me. In this "Stop thinking and jump" moment, I slipped one leg behind the bully's legs, stood up abruptly, and threw my arms out wide.

It worked! He fell backward onto the concrete. He got up quickly, cursing at me. Then he just walked away. I stood there, shaken by a hormonal cocktail of adrenaline and elation.

After that I started practicing Okinawa-te, a martial art that combined the linear strikes and kicks of Japanese karate with the flowing, circular, animal-based forms of Chinese *wushu*, under the watchful eye of my sensei, Gordon Doversola.

Acrobat Daze

At the close of that school year, Mr. Leonard announced the end of the world — my world, at least: his transfer to another middle school across the city. Next year, no Mr. Leonard, no trampoline and tumbling club. For the first time in my young life, overcome by grief, I shed tears to relieve an aching sense of loss.

Sensing my sorrow, the next weekend Mr. Leonard drove me a few miles to Burbank and parked in front of a cinder-block building whose picture window revealed a row of six ground-level trampolines. (If I'd ever imagined a heavenly realm, it would have looked like that.) Mr. Leonard then introduced me to the owners, Jess and Abby Robinson, who would become like surrogate parents to me, and Trampoline Inc., my second home.

For the next five years, every Tuesday night and Saturday morning, I'd be waiting at the door when Jess and Abby arrived to open up, and they would have to push me out at closing time. At first my parents provided round-trip transport, but later I found my own way, taking three different buses.

Jess, a former lithographer, had opened Trampoline Inc. due

to his son Dar's avid interest. But since Jess had no previous acrobatic experience, I had to figure out how to learn new moves on my own. I broke each skill into smaller parts and progressions. My trampoline buddies and I experimented, trying different ways to somersault at this acrobatic playland. I struck up a friendly rivalry with Dar, who would one day become a famous stunt performer. We dared each other to do things like one hundred back somersaults in a row.

We also played Add-On, a game in which one of us would do a single move and the next jumper would do the same move, then add another, then another, until we were doing twelve, fifteen, or even twenty different twisting somersaults in a row, testing both our endurance and our memory.

First Time, First Place

By twelve years old I'd shown enough promise that Jess and Abby flew me and Dar to San Francisco, where we got a ride to the Berkeley YMCA to perform a routine in my first official trampoline and tumbling meet. That night, after swinging on ropes from the balcony and trying other crazy stunts while laughing so hard with Dar I could hardly breathe, I crawled into my sleeping bag and fell asleep on the gym mats, unaware that a few blocks from where I slept, an old Texaco service station on the corner of Oxford Street and Hearst Avenue was waiting for me.

The next morning, the meet director announced that trampolinists had to perform ten flips in a row, staying near the center of the trampoline. After watching some other bouncers do their routines, I climbed up and started jumping, then made up ten moves in a row. The judges raised some score cards with numbers too fuzzy to make out without my glasses, which I rarely wore. They had to tell me that I'd won.

Rites of Passage

When I was fourteen, I won the California State Senior Men's Trampoline Championships in a field of college athletes. That spring also marked the beginning of a national trampoline craze. In the space of a few months, ground-level trampoline centers appeared all over the United States, attracting the attention of a *LIFE Magazine* photographer. A few friends and I ended up on the cover of the May 1960 issue, with a full-page spread showing me demonstrating a few somersaults. I hoped that some of my friends at school might see it, which would be cool.

At school that year and the next, my buddies and I would meet in the playground sandpit during lunch to try out new moves on the low and high horizontal bars — pullovers, knee circles, giant swings, and flyaway dismounts. While waiting for my turn, I looked through someone's copy of *Modern Gymnast* magazine, with photos of college gymnasts doing amazing moves. I wanted to do it all!

As an adolescent, I sometimes endured pain in pursuit of thrills: While swinging around the high bar, the heat and friction ripped chunks of skin off my palms. I punctured blisters with a needle to let them drain and heal. As a rite of passage into manliness, I sprayed my bloody rips with a substance called Tough Skin, which stung like iodine on steroids, then wrapped adhesive tape over the rips, strapped on my leather handguards, and got back to it until the bell rang for the next period.

I now aspired to join the gymnastics team at nearby John Marshall High School, hoping to perform in meets there. Even if I'd never have Superman's powers, I might at least develop the superstrength to perform an iron cross on the rings.

Chapter 3

High Aspirations

*Teachers open the door
we must enter by ourselves.*

CHINESE PROVERB

"Who's your best long horse vaulter?" Those first words, on my first day of high school, were addressed to Mr. James Bogle, our heavyset biology teacher and gymnastics coach.

"That would be Tom Whisenhunt," he replied. "He's a senior and team captain."

"Well, I'm going to beat him," I said in a show of youthful bravado.

"Really," said Mr. Bogle with a wry smile. "You can warn him yourself, so he can be on full alert." He pointed to an amused eighteen-year-old senior sitting on a stool a few feet away. Tom and I became friends that year, even as I won various honors, including the top vaulting spot on the team.

That summer, my trampoline pals and I learned to run two strides straight up a wall and turn a backward somersault. After that, we ran up and flipped from trees, mailboxes, telephone poles, and even stationary buses.

One evening I dressed up in a sweater, tie, and new slacks for a dinner-and-movie date on Hollywood Boulevard. As my date and I drove through rain showers, I casually mentioned an "interesting stunt" I'd soon show her. In the early dusk, the streets were still wet and puddled, reflecting the glare of streetlights as we walked down a side street. "Okay, here's the surprise!" I said. I ran smoothly up toward the wall and took off —

Unfortunately, due to the dim light, I'd misjudged my distance from the wall, so instead of flipping backward, I kicked out into thin air and, much like a cartoon character, remained aloft for an instant before landing flat on my back in a puddle. I lay there, gazing up at my date's mystified expression.

"I missed the wall," I wheezed, stating the obvious.

After a moment of silence, she said, "Oh, well, that was really...interesting."

I don't recall what movie we saw, only that it took the entire two hours for me to dry out.

Despite the occasional mishap, my acrobatic endeavors provided a sense of purpose and progress, but also an immersive escape from stresses at home. My teenage years were a troubling time for my big sister DeDe, whose frequent emotional outbursts, slamming of doors, and silent withdrawal left me confused and stressed. I didn't understand the source of her unhappiness.

She was the same sister who taught me dance steps for the few parties I attended; the same sister whose coaching enabled me to excel at typing, preparing me for a future in writing. I was not immune to her emotional storms, but I felt powerless to help. One time, when DeDe ran into her room sobbing, I stood outside her bedroom door crying too.

DeDe and I had some happy times as well, but I never knew

when something I'd say or do might set her off. So I withdrew inside myself and focused on my own life, finding comfort and forgetfulness in the gym and up in the air, above the trauma, drama, and angst.

Two Teachers

Each week, Ivan Smith, a witty but demanding ninth-grade English teacher, showed our class an abstract painting or played an LP of classical music, then challenged us to write a short-short story of exactly two pages inspired by the work of art. The paper had to be immaculately typed, with the right margin approximating a straight line. In other words, I had to constantly edit and change words to suit his requirements. Although my early fan fiction bore an uncanny resemblance to *The Twilight Zone*, I earned nearly straight-A grades on these writing assignments and an A at the end of the term. My performance in the class revealed that it took significant effort to produce good writing, that gymnastics wasn't my only strength, and that creative writing could be intoxicating.

It wasn't until I was in the tenth grade that another gifted teacher, Mr. Thompson, made literature come to life for me as our class read and analyzed *Mutiny on the Bounty* and took turns reading Shakespeare aloud, then Thornton Wilder's moving play *Our Town*.

As I reflect on these two teachers — Mr. Thompson and Mr. Smith — I realize how many people have mentored me: authors, elders, peers, and role models, including my father and mother, each of them a lamp lighting the way. Their guidance and encouragement prepared me for all that would follow. Even as I made the transition into adolescence, my writing initiation had begun.

Risk and Fortune

For my sixteenth birthday, I pleaded with my parents to help me buy a motorcycle. "It's way less expensive than a car and easy to park," I said.

"It's just too risky," they both replied, "but we did find a used car you might like."

When we arrived outside an apartment in Westwood, a man came out with a set of keys and pointed to a 1958 Corvette hardtop convertible. Openmouthed, I turned to my parents, who were looking at me. My expression said more than any words could.

Fresh from a tune-up by Jerry, our neighborhood auto mechanic, that Corvette took off like a rocket, the g-force pressing me back into the custom tuck-and-roll upholstery. A few days later, I pulled into Jerry's repair shop to say hello. Cutting down an alley, I sped directly toward a Ford sedan with all its wheels removed, sitting up on blocks. I hit my brakes to stop a few feet short of that Ford, but my wheels skidded on loose gravel.

Time slowed down as I *willed* my Corvette to stop, but it slid a few inches too far. My front bumper barely tapped the Ford's door — not enough to dent it but enough to tip over all four blocks supporting the vehicle. I gasped as the car's undercarriage smashed onto the concrete with a terrible crunching sound, its full weight on the driveshaft. Just then I saw Jerry's horrified face appear from inside his office, his mouth agape. He was still holding a telephone receiver to his ear.

A few minutes later, while I apologized repeatedly, Jerry estimated the damage. Then he told me that thirty seconds before I'd knocked the car off its blocks, he'd been lying face up *underneath that Ford* when he heard the phone ring.

The following week, using a chunk of my savings from working at a supermarket, I arranged to pay for dinner at a fancy restaurant for Jerry and the man who'd phoned him.

In the spring of my junior year I was contacted by several college coaches, including Harold Frey at the University of California. He flew me up to Berkeley, where I toured the landscaped campus. Coach Frey told me of the team's impressive record of a hundred dual meets in a row and numerous Pac-8 conference championships. Only the coveted NCAA team title had eluded him. He hoped I might help in that endeavor.

In my senior year I applied to Cal and was accepted. My financial aid package included a campus job cleaning the stands after football games to help pay for my tuition and books.

Chapter 4

Growing Up

I have less fear of storms
now that I'm learning
how to sail my ship.

LOUISA MAY ALCOTT

At the end of my first semester at Cal, when grades were posted, I learned that I was on academic probation. That weekend, still shaken by this news, I was asked to give a trampoline exhibition during halftime at a Cal basketball game, along with two teammates. As each of them started their routine, our assistant coach Chuck Keeney introduced them: "This is Lloyd Briggs, English major with a 3.8 grade point average." (Mild applause.) Then, "Senior Tom Fashinell, premed with a 4.0 grade point average." (More applause.) As I began my routine, Mr. Keeney said, "Dan Millman, the current world trampoline champion. With his style, who needs a grade point average?" (Applause and laughter.)

My grade point average was no laughing matter to me or to Coach Frey. If I didn't improve, I'd be ineligible to compete and might even have to leave the university. I was no stranger to failure, having failed many times when attempting new trampoline and gymnastics moves. So I knew how to respond: In a major shift of priorities, I began to apply the same rigor to my studies as I'd been doing in gymnastics. If training was a rehearsal for competitions, then studying needed to become a rehearsal for exams. I memorized information the way an actor memorizes lines, typing my scribbled notes each evening, forcing myself to organize and review the material. I read and highlighted all required books. By year's end I was off probation with a strong B-average, having proven I could hold my own among other Cal students.

I also saw a connection between physical and mental training. *In a sense, how we do anything is how we do everything*, I thought. This marked a conscious mental shift from the path of expertise, or refining skills, to the path of mastery, the moment I realized the connection between training and life.

When Coach Frey saw my improved grades, he pressed the athletic director to grant Cal's only world champion a full athletic scholarship for the next three years, lifting the financial burden from my parents' shoulders. No more cleaning up the football stadium. Now I would receive a monthly check on the first day of each month in lieu of a meal ticket and campus job. Gymnastics had become a career that supported me through my undergraduate years.

In my sophomore year our team won the conference championships, and I won my first NCAA title in vaulting. (Atop the victory stand, I flashed back to the day I'd vowed to become the best vaulter in my high school.) I ended up choosing psychology as my major, but it wasn't really a career choice. I still clung to the notion that the future would take care of itself, which was an exceptionally wise (or uniquely foolish) approach to life planning.

In my junior year at Cal, I was invited to teach trampoline and tumbling clinics to young gymnasts during winter break. When one of my students remarked, "You'd be a great coach, Dan," I shrugged it off, believing I should set my sights on a profession or…something like that. Years later, Lily Tomlin would capture my hazy goals when she said, "I always wanted to be *somebody*, but maybe I should have been more specific."

When I volunteered to teach a Saturday morning children's tumbling class at the Berkeley Y, I brought in a big box filled with all the medals, plaques, and trophies I'd won over the years so the Y could get them reengraved and pass them on to the youngsters.

Crossing Paths with the Dead

"Would you put on this ski mask," the man asked, "and do some trampoline flips while strobe lights flash?"

"Sure," I said, pointing up to a walkway about twenty feet above us. "Would you like me to start my routine by diving off that balcony?" He liked the idea, so I donned the mask, did the dive, and performed about twenty flips with twists while nearly blinded by the flashing light. I then hopped off the trampoline and melted into the crowd, wandering through a surreal scene before heading back to Berkeley.

My little performance was arranged between Coach Frey and Stewart Brand, organizer of the 1966 San Francisco Trips Festival, a seminal convergence of performance art and psychedelic celebration, with readings by Ken Kesey plus the debut of a band (formerly the Warlocks) newly christened as the Grateful Dead. It was also a large-scale acid test held before LSD was outlawed nine months later. In an interview with Gabe Meline for KQED/NPR in 2016, Stewart Brand offered the following commentary:

NPR: *As far as specific snapshots go, when you think of the Trips Festival today, what memories come immediately to mind?*

Brand: I guess my favorite moment is the one that I designed, in which I hired an Olympic-level gymnast named Dan Millman. I think it was in the peak of weirdness on Saturday. We dragged a trampoline that I borrowed from San Francisco State College out into the middle space in Longshoremen's Hall and set up a series of linked strobes around it. And then suddenly, from the balcony, he comes diving through the air in a ski mask, lands on the trampoline, and proceeds to go up and up and up doing Olympic-level triple somersaults and multiple twists and whatnot. All with the flash-flash-flash of the strobe lights, and with people standing around wondering if what they were seeing was there in the world or there in their mind, and they were sort of checking with each other: "Do you see what I see?"

He did a beautiful performance, which can't have been easy with a strobe light and a ski mask on. He did enough of those [somersaults] to blow your mind. Then he snuck off into the crowd and we removed the trampoline and that was that. I paid him $50, I think.

Two Seconds in Show Biz

The school year ended with mixed outcomes: On the bright side, I'd maintained respectable grades, but in the gymnastics arena, the University of Washington, buoyed by a home crowd and local judges, edged us out of a conference championship. Many spectators and several other coaches questioned the outcome. This bitter disappointment only strengthened our resolve to win our first national collegiate team title the following year.

One great thing about sport: There's always the next season.

Early that summer, the US Gymnastics Federation (USGF) invited my friend and teammate Sid Freudenstein and me, both potential Olympians, to participate in a two-week training camp at Penn State University. Knowing I was being evaluated by great coaches inspired me to new heights of daring. As the wild card of the group, relying on innovation (and occasional miracles), I attempted several moves that no one to my knowledge had accomplished before. At the end of the camp, the USGF decided to send Sid and me to Ljubljana, Yugoslavia (now Slovenia), to train with elite gymnasts at the World Gymnastics Championships, for international exposure, just before the school year would begin.

Everything was falling into place. In the best shape of my life, I felt primed for my final year of collegiate competition. After all that Coach Frey had done for me, I wanted to help deliver his dream of a national team championship before I shifted my focus to the US Olympic Trials.

Near the end of the summer, despite my parents' concerns, I sold the Corvette and bought a Triumph 500cc motorcycle. And just when I thought it couldn't get any better, I was chosen, along with my longtime trampoline buddy Steve Lerner, to perform some gymnastics stunt work in a scene being filmed at the Malibu Yacht Club for a forgettable movie called *Don't Make Waves* starring Tony Curtis, Claudia Cardinale, and Sharon Tate. Each morning I rode my purring Triumph up the Pacific Coast Highway to the set with my guitar strapped to the luggage rack. During downtime, stunt performer Russ Saunders and I spotted Tony Curtis in a handheld safety belt so he could learn a back somersault on the trampoline.

After my quick brush with Hollywood, the final days of

summer passed quickly. Since I planned to ride the Triumph north to Berkeley the day before I'd fly to Yugoslavia, I decided to visit my sister in West Los Angeles. As I grabbed my helmet and headed downstairs, my dad called out the window, "Be careful, Dan!"

"I will," I called back, revving the bike, feeling cool in my gymnastics T-shirt and faded Levi's.

Chapter 5

A Change of Plans

Numberless are your teachers.
The opportunity offered you is your teacher;
the agony inflicted on you is your teacher;
every wrench at the heartstrings
that makes the tears flow is your teacher.

BAULS' VERSE

When I left my sister's apartment, the streetlights were turning on in the early dusk. Invigorated by the cool evening air, I headed north on Western Avenue, where I noticed a light-colored Cadillac ahead, facing me, waiting to make a left turn. I slowed — a precaution that may have saved my life. Just as I entered the intersection, the driver gunned the Caddy, turning left directly in front of me.

I slammed on the brakes and glimpsed a frozen image of the driver's horrified face. With a terrible slam and the sound of tinkling glass, everything sped up, then the world turned black. A witness said that my body somersaulted over the vehicle, then landed with a thud. When I came to, moments later, I was lying on my back on the concrete.

As I regained consciousness, I looked down and saw the white bone sticking out through the torn leather of my left shoe. Then I felt a searing, red-hot vise crushing my right thigh. I stifled a scream until the pain overwhelmed me. Looking skyward, I saw a small circle of concerned bystanders hovering over me. Their voices seemed far away. Then a siren's wail grew louder. Hands held my head, removed my helmet, lifted me onto a stretcher.

I passed in and out of agonized dreams: a vague impression of the inside of the ambulance racing through a time warp into the Los Angeles Orthopaedic Hospital's ER. The on-call surgeon was apparently near the end of shift. "I'm bushed," I heard him say.

Moaning as my right leg throbbed and spasmed, I tried to slow my rapid, shallow breathing. My ashen face, cold sweat, and rising nausea signaled I was in shock, which meant the ER doc couldn't give me any sedation. So I was fully conscious when he pulled out each of the dislocated toes of my left foot, popping them back into their respective sockets, and then pushed my left big toe bone back into place, stitching the wound closed. Then, turning his full attention to my primary injury, the surgeon drilled a long screw through my lower leg just below the knee, connected a cable, and hung weights to create traction, stretching my thigh to reduce the spasms, taking pressure off the bone, which had shattered into about thirty fragments.

In a state of shock and disorientation, I asked the doctor if I could still fly overseas in two or three days to train at the World Championships. His only response was: "In six months, with some work, you should be able to walk normally again."

Soon after, Mom, Dad, and my sister DeDe appeared in the hospital room, looking pale, their faces anguished. That's when the devastating reality caught up with me. I fought off tears of self-pity until after my parents and sister departed. Then I fell into a restless sleep through that long night.

I called Coach Frey the next morning. Taking a deep breath, I told him the news. For a few moments, I heard only silence. Then he wished me a good recovery and said he'd notify the athletic department. "Your main job right now is to heal, Dan. I'll check back in next week." I could sense his disappointment. When I purchased that motorcycle, I'd been thinking about my self-image, not about the team or Coach or my parents.

Later that day the orthopedist explained that I'd need to choose between six months in traction or surgery. For once, it wasn't hard to decide.

A few days before the surgery, a physician friend visited my hospital room and gave me a booklet about the benefits of a vegetarian diet — how it was possible to ingest plenty of protein without animal flesh. Up to that point, I'd never thought much about what I ate. Now, healing was a priority. The booklet made so much sense that I resolved to stop eating animals. By following a lighter, nonmeat diet, I'd likely be healthier for many years to come. Only later would I learn of the wider benefits of a primarily plant-based diet for our planet.

The following week, the surgeon sliced a long red line deep into the side of my right thigh, cutting through the muscles that had worked so well for me. He removed bone from my pelvis and grafted it to the shattered bone, then he hammered a titanium nail down the center of my femur from the hip nearly to the knee to serve as an internal cast.

When I awoke, the pain was so intense that I needed an injection of Demerol, a strong painkiller with sedative effects, every four hours, after which I fell into a deep sleep until I was again awakened by the pain. Over the next several days I fell into a rhythm of drug-induced sleep, then pain, then sleep, until the pain finally subsided several days later. Nothing, I discovered, is more pleasurable than the cessation of pain.

Only later did a nurse inform me that a young man named Steve Hug had visited. I'd met Steve, a brilliant high school gymnast, when we'd both performed routines at the Santa Monica Beach Gymfest. Emotionally vulnerable due to the painkillers, I remember a nurse's account of Steve sitting quietly at my bedside for nearly an hour while I slept.

A Different Life

On the day of my release, after three weeks flat on my back, I nearly passed out the first time I stood up. I wouldn't need an external cast but would depend on crutches for at least three months. I'd lost so much weight that my pants wouldn't stay up when I first put them on. After crutch training on stairs and a farewell to the on-duty nurses, I was good to go.

A fresh breeze caressed my face on the rare, smog-free day as I crutched through the hospital parking lot to my parents' car. The wind carried scents I'd forgotten. Chirping birds in a nearby tree, mixed with the sound of traffic, created a symphony for my freshly awakened senses. As odd as it seemed under the circumstances, I was in a blissful state of mind, free of the self-imposed pressure to excel that had driven me for years — a pressure I had only noticed due to its sudden absence.

Despite this painful disruption, I considered how much worse the injury could have been. I had no head or spinal injury. I found peace in the space of uncertainty, not knowing whether I'd ever return to my previous state of fitness. I'd have to do what I could and see what unfolded.

As soon as I arrived home, I sat on a stool in the shower and let the hot water wash away the painful memories of the past three weeks, and the reality of all those people I'd disappointed: Coach, my teammates, my parents, and, finally, myself.

I stayed with my parents for a few days, resting in the hot sun and swimming slowly through the shallow end of their small swimming pool, painfully forcing my sutured leg muscles to work. I ate sparingly, according to my taste and hunger: fresh vegetables and fruit, yogurt, nuts, eggs, whole grains, and cheese, slowly regaining my vitality.

Without the bulletproof bravado typical of twenty-somethings, I now felt quieter and more reflective, grateful for the support of the medical staff and my parents. Not since childhood had I needed to rely on others in this way. That injury had expanded my perspectives about what really mattered and generated larger questions about life.

Physically, I was disabled. The surgeon had measured my leg lengths and found that the right, operative leg was a quarter inch shorter than the left. Also, my right leg below the surgery site was externally rotated fifteen degrees — the odds were stacked against walking normally much less rejoining the team.

With the fall term already underway, there was no point in returning to Berkeley just yet. When friends invited me to stay with them for a few weeks at their home in Santa Monica, five blocks from the beach, I gratefully accepted.

So, for the next four weeks, I crutched my way to the beach each morning, carrying a beach towel, three juggling balls, surgical tubing for strength work, and a book, alternately reading and strength training. I spent several hours each day sweating in the hot sun. I pressed up to handstands again and again, puffing with exertion until every muscle had worked to its limit. Then I hopped one-legged into the shallow surf and sat dreaming of lofty somersaults until the salt water washed my sweat and soaring dreams into the sea.

During those four weeks I was one of the beach regulars who made the sea and sand a way of life. Malcolm the masseur would tell jokes; Doc, the Rand Corporation think-tank wiz, would drop by my spot every day and talk with me about politics and women. Mostly about women. Meanwhile, my upper-body muscles were as hard and defined as a marble statue, but my right leg still looked like a stick.

By the time I was ready to return to Cal, Sid had already flown overseas and trained with the world's top gymnasts. Now the team was preparing for the coming season. My own plans had scattered like bowling pins.

My Life as a Ghost

That December, back in Berkeley in the closing weeks of 1966, I found a tiny studio room in a boardinghouse a few blocks from the gym. Glad to be self-sufficient again, I managed to navigate the carpeted stairs on crutches while carrying a laundry bag or a few grocery items. The solitude suited my monklike, contemplative bubble.

The first time I returned to the vitality of the gymnastics room, made strange by my absence, I saw new faces as well as the familiar ones. Rick, Sid, and a few other teammates drew near. Glancing at the crutches, they commented on the stupidity of "racing a motorcycle down Hollywood Boulevard" (which I hadn't done). Herb chastised me for sabotaging our chances of a national team championship his senior year. I'd expected nothing less — far better than a show of sympathy.

Each morning after that, gripping my crutches tightly, I'd

make my way to the gym and train on the weight machines, then fall exhausted into the swimming pool. Assisted by the water's buoyancy, I walked back and forth, always to the point of pain, but no further. Afterward, I'd lie on the lawn behind the gym, stretching my muscles to retain the suppleness I'd need for future training. Finally, I rested, reading in the library, often drifting into a light sleep.

Navigating slowly around campus, I felt invisible, a ghost-like presence — there yet not there, on campus but not a student, in the gym but not on the team. As everyone else studied for final exams, I trained alone in the weight room or in a corner of the gymnastics room, stretching and working my upper-body strength as my teammates swung on the bars and tumbled and vaulted, preparing for a season I would view from the stands.

I donated the crutches, bought a cane, and began testing my right leg's capacity, starting with five-pound weights, finishing with a light, tentative massage.

Because I wasn't currently enrolled as a full-time college student, I was called to a draft physical as the United States was drawn ever deeper into the Vietnam War. When I showed the X-ray of the nail down the length of my thigh, I was reclassified as unfit to serve.

In mid-December, before winter break, a slim, red-haired woman with a pretty face behind wire-rim glasses, dropped by the gym to watch the team practice. She immediately caught my eye. Soon after that, we exchanged a few words. Her name was Linda, and she was a first-year student. She invited me to dinner at her apartment. By the time I departed, it was nearly three o'clock in the morning.

On my way home, at the corner of Oxford and Hearst, destiny waited under a starlit sky.

A Chance Meeting

Hobbling home with my cane, I turned my head toward the well-lit office of an all-night Texaco service station, which stood out in a dark wilderness of closed shops. As I entered, seeking a snack from a vending machine, I met the lone night attendant. His unlined face, clear eyes, and relaxed manner made it difficult to guess his age. He seemed glad for the company, so we struck up a conversation that somehow led to musings on the nature of reality. Due to my receptive state, maybe a cosmic compensation for the motorcycle crash, doors opened in my mind.

I recall few details of that conversation, but the man's voice and presence stirred something in me that I couldn't name, giving birth to someone I'd name Socrates, after the ancient Athenian philosopher. Following our meeting, I would never again make assumptions about anyone's wisdom or awareness based solely on the role they played in life.

After I departed, never to see that old mechanic again, word strings appeared in my mind, which turned into a ten-page poem I scrawled as soon as I returned to my room. The poem, inspired by our chance meeting, was lost or discarded over the passage of time, but a few phrases would form the seeds of an autobiographical novel fourteen years later.

Linda and I saw more of each other that spring of 1967, until she decided to leave Cal and move to Los Angeles to find work. After that we spoke on the phone often and traded a few letters.

Chapter 6

Shifting Sands

I have learned silence from the talkative,
toleration from the intolerant,
and kindness from the unkind.
Strange that I am not also
grateful to these teachers.

KAHLIL GIBRAN

My friend and teammate Herb Solomon captured the zeitgeist of the 1960s during our college years in a reflective letter he wrote to our team just prior to our fifty-year reunion:

> Campus life was incredibly cool: the Civil Rights Movement, Stokely Carmichael, the Vietnam War protests and Free Speech Movement, Alpert and Leary, Dylan, the Beatles, the Stones, sex and psychotropic herbs, the Fugs, the Airplane, the Dead, Country Joe and the Fish, Ken Kesey and the Merry Pranksters, Haight-Ashbury, hippies, acid, and the Fillmore — they all came together into the Berkeley vortex. The UC campus felt like the center of the universe, and in a certain sense it was.

Even while immersed in the color and drama of the late '60s, my attention had shifted inward, into a universe parallel to but separate from popular fashion and ideology, carried by spiritual currents that would change over the ensuing decades. I was the horseback rider who, when asked where I was going, would answer, "You'll have to ask the horse." That steed of my psyche was drawn into unexpected territory, out of step and out of time, yearning for the timeless.

During my belated final year at Cal, surrounded by "Make Love, Not War" ideals and tie-dyed shirts at every turn, I passed through Sproul Plaza with a backdrop of growing protests against the Vietnam War. I opposed the war but avoided crowds. I focused on studies, rehabilitation, and training to turn a dream into reality.

The team completed a respectable season without me but lost their first home competition in a decade. No one on the team, including me, knew whether I'd compete again. I still walked with an odd gait, throwing one hip to the side due to the top section of the long nail in my right femur irritating my hip.

Still, I pushed onward, moving from weight training to more handstands and some swing work on rings and the high bar, dropping slowly from the apparatus, landing on one leg. When I did my first giant swings around the high bar, Sid and Tom stayed close by, ready to catch me. We'd always had a close-knit team, a band of brothers, but now they sometimes acted like mother hens. This only made me take more risks, like doing back somersaults, taking off and landing on one leg.

Lucy in the Sky with Diamonds

Now acutely aware of my mortality after the motorcycle crash had disrupted my life, I felt a growing urge to know more about inner worlds and higher possibilities. Since LSD was said to bring profound understanding of a reality invisible to the everyday mind, I decided to take a deep dive into my psyche.

After a classmate hooked me up with a tab of lysergic acid diethylamide, I asked my teammate Herb how to prepare.

"Have you ever smoked grass, Dan?"

"No. I don't like the idea of inhaling smoke into my lungs."

"Have you ever been drunk?"

"Nope. Never developed a taste for beer or wine. Maybe it's a genetic thing."

"Well, I suggest you get stoned or intoxicated before you trip on LSD."

So I smoked some weed. It was the first time I'd truly appreciated classical music or the munchies — enhanced taste, sound, and pseudomeaning, a kind of "Whoa dude" profundity that faded once the high wore off. Whatever goes up comes down. The high left me with a familiar dissatisfaction. I could see how I might get high again, and again, and still end up in the same place, which seemed pointless. I also felt an instinctive aversion to using mind-altering substances for casual, recreational use. (I'd smoke or ingest pot a few more times, but it was never really my thing.)

To prepare myself for the LSD journey (the word *trip* seemed too trivial), I read *The Psychedelic Experience: A Manual Based on the Tibetan Book of the Dead*, coauthored by Timothy Leary, Ralph Metzner, and Richard Alpert. As Leary famously once said, "The worst thing that can happen to you after taking LSD is that you come back the same person that you were."

About this time, Ray Hadley, a graduate student in psychology and an elite gymnast who trained with the team, told me he had a spare bedroom in his apartment on University Avenue. After moving in, I'd sometimes sit on the rooftop of the building, above the sounds of traffic, and read and mentally prepare for the coming journey.

I asked Ray to keep an eye on me while he spent the morning reading the Sunday paper. In that safe, secure setting, with Indian sitar music playing in the background, I ingested the tab. Ray later told me that I had lain absolutely still on the couch for the next four hours, during which I'd visited unexplored psychic spaces, soaring through the cosmos within. With LSD as my travel agent, I surrendered to whatever visions appeared, like vivid dream images: floating in space, splitting into a million crystal shards, recombining, dissolving, experiencing absolute terror, dark night of the soul, death of the ego, and then a rebirth, seeing the divine everywhere, as everything took on a sense of the profound meaning expressed by William Blake: "To see a World in a Grain of Sand. And a Heaven in a Wild Flower. Hold Infinity in the palm of your hand. And Eternity in an hour." At some point during this magical mystery tour, I melted into the soil, the trees, the mountains, the rivers, the sky, in a unified vision of possibility.

That tiny tab of LSD revealed a nonordinary reality that transcended and illuminated my everyday state of mind to display a numinous dimension, a spiritual reality in which Dan Millman was but a raindrop of consciousness in an ocean of bliss. My psychedelic experience brought to light new possibilities, shifted my priorities, and later would inspire the visionary journeys I described a decade later in *Way of the Peaceful Warrior*. But, as psychologist Richard Alpert (later known as Ram Dass) had discovered, LSD might point the way, but only sustained spiritual practice could lead to transcendence.

Quickening

After my LSD experience, which marked the conscious beginning of my search for illumination, I began browsing bookstore shelves on philosophy, psychology, and religion. After wading through a few classics, I gravitated toward modern writers like Alan Watts and Aldous Huxley, who wrote in ways I could understand better than the arcane language written for earlier times and cultures. I encountered bohemian souls on Telegraph Avenue who proclaimed their Truth, Teacher, or Path, but it wasn't my nature to jump onto someone else's bandwagon. An inner voice whispered, *Onward!* as it prodded me toward an unknown destination.

That summer, a year after my motorcycle crash, the surgeon removed the nail from my femur, enabling me to walk normally again with a lift in one shoe. For the first time, I thought: *I may have a chance of rejoining my team.* Clinging to that hope, I worked to complete my studies and my final gymnastics season. My aim was laser focused on the NCAA championships, a long-sought dream of Coach Frey. I couldn't let Coach or the team down again.

On my last summer break, in August 1967, I visited Linda in Los Angeles and, at Santa Monica Beach, as we lay on a blanket in the warm sun, I surprised both of us when, on impulse, I asked her to marry me. We hadn't known each other that long and hardly even knew ourselves. She was nineteen, and I was twenty-one.

Before that moment, I'd never thought about marriage. I puzzled over it, trying to fathom my motives. Maybe I was influenced by Rick, who had married his longtime sweetheart a few months earlier, and Sid, who had just gotten engaged. Or maybe I just needed to make *some* kind of decision, to take charge of my life. Only later did it occur to me that the advice "Stop thinking and jump!" might not apply to every decision. Now the die was cast. After a civil ceremony in Berkeley, we rented an apartment.

In September, Linda found work as a bank teller, and I enrolled in my final term at Cal. In January 1968, Linda told me she was pregnant. I accepted this as welcome news before turning back to a mission begun years before: the NCAA championships.

During my final term, recalling the creative pleasure I'd

experienced writing short stories a decade earlier, I signed up for a correspondence course through the Famous Writers School. After reading their four comprehensive textbooks, I sent in assigned fiction and nonfiction pieces, which were returned to me with editorial markups, showing me how to improve the work. This would be my only formal training — an excellent introduction to producing quality work. Several years later a scandal arose about the school's questionable business practices, but my own experience was positive.

Then, just three weeks before the NCAA championships, I graduated from UC Berkeley in March 1968 as Senior Athlete of the Year. And because NCAA rules allowed recent graduates to complete their final athletic season, I would rejoin my team in Tucson, Arizona, for the culminating event of many years of training.

Looking back on my four undergraduate years, I see myself as the archetypal student: smart and dumb, idealistic and cynical, compassionate and self-centered, insecure and full of myself. I was, after all, then still a teenager, growing toward adulthood and gaining perspective. In college I'd tested myself against structured challenges before taking on a career or long-term relationship, woefully unprepared for either one. I'd hoped to get educated, get laid, maybe even get religion. Perhaps a part of me wanted to save the world or just save (or find) myself. And, like many college students, I was sustained by the hubris of youth.

Immersive physical training and my accident had also bestowed a measure of humility as I stumbled and fell and got up again. Participating in sport taught me that progress is hard-earned, and happens not overnight but over time. Nonathletes sometimes appear to have the luxury of adopting a style or persona, but there's no pretense in sport. I strove and struggled, failing again and again, until I finally experienced fleeting moments of satisfaction.

The Wheel of Fortune

Linda and I moved to Los Angeles with about five hundred dollars left in our bank account, I looked in the classified job ads and found work selling life insurance, feeling as if I were stepping into someone else's life. With a baby due, and the need to make a living, I had to relinquish my Olympic ambitions.

In early April, I joined my team for the last time in a closely contested match with Southern Illinois University for the NCAA team championship. After three events, Cal trailed SIU by nearly two points, a significant gap, but every one of us hit solid routines, and by the last event, the horizontal bar, we were in striking distance.

Southern Illinois still had a full point lead, but our team was on fire. I was the last man up, ready for the final routine of my competitive career. Memories flashed through my mind: the days of pain after my thighbone was splintered, the doctor's admonition to forget about gymnastics, regaining my strength, running up into the hills...

I felt a surge of power, then icy calm — my mind clear, my body tingling. The arena was silent as I jumped up to the bar and drove my legs upward. I swung, vaulted, twisted, released again, and caught the shining pipe. Dissolving into the purity of motion, I added a move I'd only done in practice, then swung faster, releasing the bar for the dismount, a piked double flyaway — spinning, floating in space, in the hands of fate. I kicked open, stretched my body, and thudded to the mat in a solid landing.

Then, pandemonium. Coach Frey grabbed my hand and shook it wildly, refusing to let go in his rapture. As my teammates leaped to their feet, I heard applause thundering in the distance.

It was over. A long-awaited goal was accomplished. But the applause didn't feel the same anymore. My search for victory finished, I retired on a high note. After a raucous team farewell overshadowed by a sense of loss at our parting, I flew back to Los Angeles. Laying my head back on the pillow as the jet started its descent, I imagined myself living in a camper van, parking at scenic overlooks, and writing when I wasn't visiting friends around the country. I awoke with a start when the wheels touched down. And for the briefest moment, I wondered: *What happened to the life I might have lived?*

Six weeks later, on a Saturday evening, I sat in the stands of UCLA's Pauley Pavilion and cheered for Sid as he and other gymnast friends each earned a place on the US Olympic Team. The top spot went to sixteen-year-old Steve Hug, the young gymnast I'd once met at the beach and who, the nurse had told me, had sat quietly beside my hospital bed while I slept.

After the Olympic Trials, I drove up to Sacramento and dropped Linda off at her parents' place, then drove to Berkeley and visited Harmon Gym to see Coach Frey. Surprised to see me, he said, "Dan, just this morning I heard that Stanford is looking for a new gymnastics coach. Why don't you call the athletic director?"

Two days later, I was offered the coaching position. Half of my modest salary came from coaching and half from teaching physical education classes, but we would manage.

Soon after, our daughter Holly was born. We were now a family.

Chapter 7

Coaching Years

*A coach is someone whose hindsight
can become your foresight.*

ANONYMOUS

At Stanford I faced the daunting task of transforming what was essentially a group operating at high school level into a top collegiate men's team. Prior to my arrival, I learned that most of the team members attended workouts "as their studies allowed," treating workouts as a recreational study break two or three days a week. The upgrade began at our first meeting, when I announced, "Beginning tomorrow, guys, workouts are five days a week, three hours each day."

Craig, Stanford's only standout all-around performer (who might even have made the Cal team), raised his hand and told me that my new schedule wasn't going to work for him because he had a heavy academic load. As a UC grad, I knew about academic loads and also about the requirements of training. This was a critical moment: I shared my aspirations for the program and my experience at Cal. "Anyone who wants to be on this new team needs to meet the standards," I said. "No exceptions." So Craig opted out. It was a sacrifice on many levels, but the standards held.

The guys who stuck it out did the best they could in a dismal first season. I'd have to build from the ground up. To help attract more experienced gymnasts to Stanford, I composed an article for *International Gymnast Magazine* titled "The Art of Gymnastics," reflecting my growing interest in Zen, Taoism, and Eastern philosophy, highlighting the internal benefits of training and its relevance in everyday life.

I'd already developed (and could teach) the physical qualities that contributed to an athlete's talent for sport. Now, returning to the gym in my new role, I wondered: *What are the mental and emotional qualities that contribute to our talent for living?* That question led me to further insights that shifted my style of coaching as I grasped how training mirrors everyday life.

Since I no longer actively trained in the gym, I started running to stay in shape, beginning with a half a mile and extending the runs until I could do five miles. Every run hurt because I pushed myself to my limits, as always. But when one of my gymnastics students asked if I'd like to go for a run with him and a few friends, their relaxed pace surprised me. I could carry on a conversation and actually enjoy running! I recalled a similar revelation the first time I experienced a relaxed golf swing and watched the ball fly.

The next day, on entering the gym, I found Brian, our team captain, lying on his back and stretching his hamstrings by pulling a straight leg toward his chest. As I walked past him, I heard him muttering to himself: "Oh! I hate this. It hurts so much!"

I turned to Brian and asked, "Who's doing it to you?" We both laughed as he got the point.

Many intense athletes end up with injuries and burn out, so I advised the team to aim for 80 percent of maximum effort. It might take them a little longer to improve, but they'd stay healthier and enjoy the process of learning in a more relaxed way. This advice runs counter to the "no pain no gain" school. There are moments to go all out, but over time, the wisdom of a more relaxed approach paid physical, emotional, and psychological dividends.

My morning-to-night focus on the team brought a corresponding inattention to my marriage. During my Stanford years, that gap would lead us to seeing a marriage counselor, then to several trial separations, which left my mind and emotions in turmoil.

Then one day a possible solution to my troubled mind literally knocked on my door.

A Monk at the Door

A Zen *roshi* (meditation teacher) visited me in the Old Pavilion and asked me if I would give permission for him to bring a small circle of *zazen* (sitting meditation) practitioners into the gym early mornings to meditate on the floor exercise mat. I said they were most welcome and ended up joining in. Practitioners of *zazen* like to call it "just sitting." I was given simple instructions about proper posture and watching (sometimes counting) the breaths. When thoughts intruded, I turned my attention back to the inbreath...and outbreath...

A few weeks into zazen practice, I drove to Berkeley, where I was also initiated into Transcendental Meditation, which uses an internal sound (a mantra), rather than the breath, as an object of attention. After a preparatory talk, the teacher whispered my mantra, a Sanskrit word, into my ear. I was instructed to sit for twenty minutes, twice daily. That first meditation at the Berkeley center was so deep it seemed that only a few short minutes had passed when I heard the soft gong. I found TM a graceful, effort-less practice. As soon as I noticed thoughts appearing in my field of awareness, I turned my attention back to the mantra.

I experimented with these two approaches. Sometimes I practiced *zazen*. Other times I practiced the TM mantra method. Neither approach could solve my relationship dilemma, but they both afforded some distance from my whirling thoughts. At first I practiced TM twice each day for the prescribed twenty min-utes, but as the months passed I shifted to once a day and then occasionally, until other events, practices, and circumstances intervened.

In this early exploration, I realized that the primary benefit of sitting meditation wasn't quieting the mind but rather quiet-ing the body. Then, as the body became deeply settled, so did the mind. These insights filtered into my approach to coaching and teaching.

The Pleasure of Beginners

Building a strong team monopolized much of my energy and attention, but I didn't neglect my beginning trampoline and gymnastics classes. In fact, I enjoyed teaching these enthusiastic novices more, in some ways, than working with the team. During the competitive season, the team and I felt an underlying pres-sure, as would any athlete or artist preparing for a performance. But the motley group of men and women in my beginning classes were delighted with any progress, with each new skill. There was no external pressure, no identity or self-worth riding on their modest achievements, just the joy of learning. It was a feeling I tried to reawaken in the team as well.

Teaching beginners helped me hone my teaching skills. I can still recall my first day of my first class, starting with the easiest skill: I demonstrated a forward roll by squatting down, placing my palms on the mat, then ducking my head as I extended my legs, then completing the roll up to a standing position. I turned to the class and was about to say, "Now you try it," when I saw their puzzled, uncertain looks. One of them asked, "Um, but how do I get my butt up over my head?"

I realized that I was going to have to break the skill down into smaller parts. After mastering the parts, they could put them all together, applying the method of progressions that as kids my friends and I had done at Trampoline Inc. a decade before. Using this approach, we built toward basic routines on trampoline, floor exercise, and the other apparatus by semester's end.

Dark Clouds and Illuminations

Soon after I applied for and was granted a faculty resident apartment in a Stanford residence hall, Linda developed her own social life, relieving me of a burden I could not or would not fulfill. We separated once, then again, in the spring of my third year. Dark emotional clouds overshadowed my remaining time at the university. I felt so much stress that any small hangnail or paper cut would quickly become infected, ample evidence of the interaction of mind, body, and emotions.

Meanwhile, I delved deeper into my coaching and teaching work. For the team members who got rattled at competitions, I called a meeting after workout, and said, "If I asked you to walk across a balance beam one foot from the floor, you'd find that easy to accomplish. But let's say I stretched the same beam between the rooftops of two fifty-story buildings and asked you to walk across. How many of you would find that equally simple?" No one's hand went up.

"What's the difference?" I asked.

"If you fall, you die," one of them said.

"True enough, but it's the same beam, the same skill. The challenge is in your mind."

Seeing them nod, I continued: "Many of you treat practice as the low beam and competition as the high beam. So from now on, each time you perform a routine in practice, pretend it's the high beam. And when competing, imagine it's the low beam. Just relax, and strive for excellence."

Soon after that talk, one of the guys on the team invited me to his dorm room and put a record on his turntable. The next words I heard were those of former Harvard psychology professor Richard Alpert describing his transformation into a spiritual teacher and author of the spiritual classic *Be Here Now*. Unlike his friend and Harvard colleague Timothy Leary, who'd become the high priest of LSD, Alpert had left psychedelics behind to devote his life to his guru, Neem Karoli Baba, who gave him the name Ram Dass and showed him a nonchemical approach to spiritual growth.

By 1971, Oprah Winfrey had just turned seventeen, her sights set on hosting a radio show. Nineteen-year-old Marianne Williamson was hoping for something bigger. Deepak Chopra was a medical intern. Wayne Dyer was a practicing psychologist planning to write his first book. Scott Peck was a United States Army psychiatrist. *A Course in Miracles* did not yet exist, nor did EMDR (eye movement desensitization and reprocessing). The first est training was only a seed in the mind of Werner Erhard. That same year, I sat in my little office and paged through a new $1.65 Ballantine book by Severin Peterson, *A Catalog of the Ways People Grow*. And I wanted it all.

During this period I happened to read an article in *Look* magazine by a self-described athletic revolutionary named Jack Scott, a PhD in sociology and sport. That article was an odd blend of progressive ideas and incendiary notions. Curious, I phoned Mr. Scott, introduced myself, and shared my candid impressions of his article. Later, we met for dinner to continue our conversation. I liked his ideas about college athletes, and he appreciated my approach as well. This seemingly chance meeting would soon have an impact on my future.

Over the coming months I sat with the Zen group in the mornings and read related books nearly every evening. Filled with a desire to share emerging insights, I taught an undergraduate special course titled Life as an Art, reflecting my expanding interests in Asian teachings and life's bigger picture and promise. The students seemed to enjoy this different sort of offering with its Eastern perspectives and a creative project in lieu of a final exam.

Revisiting the Warrior's Way

About this time I revisited martial arts training, devoting several evenings a week to aikido, a flowing art resonant with my emerging values and aesthetics. I appreciated how the founder, Morihei Ueshiba, named it "the art of peace," and how its circular movements were primarily defensive in nature. Aikido felt like a practice of graceful living.

One evening, while practicing with my sensei, Robert Nadeau, I asked whether aikido was an effective self-defense art. In his typically gruff voice, he answered, "If you want self-defense, get a gun." He then proceeded to slip my punch and body-slam me to the mat — making a point, I supposed.

Even after I eventually earned a *shodan*, a first-degree black belt, I couldn't imagine applying well-rehearsed aikido techniques done with compliant partners in a chaotic, real-world, high-adrenal confrontation.

While I now understood the difference between martial arts and real-world self-defense, the fulfillment of my childhood quest for practical self-defense would have to wait another three decades.

New Perspectives

As my worldview expanded, I introduced the team to what I called Zen gymnastics, reminding them that they weren't training just to win competitions but to master themselves — that gymnastics was a dynamic meditation, a means to access elevated states of awareness. (This may not seem like a radical idea today, but it was cutting edge in the early 1970s.) I added, "I'm not asking you to devote your life to training; I'm asking you to dedicate training to your life. And don't aim for success, which isn't in your control; just aim for excellence, which is."

I went on to share my view that gymnastics was a performance art shoehorned into the mold of a competitive sport, in which judges turned creative routines into numbers, then compared the numbers to see who was best. "Approach competition in a lighthearted way to keep the athletic department happy, but never take competition, or yourselves, too seriously."

During a dual meet, the USC coach pulled me aside and, in a teasing tone, said, "Dan, I heard a rumor that you have your team members meditate before competitions."

"Of course not," I said. "I have them meditate *during* competitions."

This easygoing emphasis and reduced external pressures to win only improved the team's performance. It also amplified their sense of meaning as training became a path of personal growth relevant to their larger lives outside the gym.

The team easily outscored USC for the first time ever. (I

couldn't entirely ignore scores since they made for good copy on *The Stanford Daily* sports page and kept the athletic department happy.) Later that year, Cal narrowly edged out our young team to win the conference championships. But that spring the program attracted several promising new recruits, including my young friend and Olympian Steve Hug, who would win his first of three consecutive NCAA all-around titles.

After four years of striving, our team was poised on the threshold of greatness.

Life Isn't Always Fair

If life were based on merit alone, it would be more predictable. We could simply work hard and do well. But luck and timing can go either way. Just after the competitive season ended, the assistant athletic director called me into his office. I knocked on his door, thinking, *Maybe he wants to acknowledge all my efforts and the team's accomplishments.*

He got right to the point, informing me of a new policy for the following school year: Only physical educators with master's degrees could teach activity classes. Stunned, I thought about what this meant — first, it cut my already-modest salary in half, and, second, I was no longer authorized to teach any gymnastics classes, which I so enjoyed.

"You're welcome to secure a part-time job off campus," he added.

That summer, as I considered my options, spinning the wheel of fortune once again, I got a call from Jack Scott, whom I'd met a few months earlier. Now the athletic director and chairman of the physical education department at Oberlin College in Ohio, he asked if I might consider joining the PE faculty as an assistant professor. Compensation was almost double that of my original Stanford salary. After discussing this opportunity with Linda, and visiting Oberlin, I accepted the position. Ever the optimist, I thought the move and new environs might renew our relationship.

I typed a letter to each member of my team, explaining the reasons for my departure, and let them know that I'd recommended an excellent new coach. I expressed my confidence that they would do well in their studies, their training, and their larger lives.

Chapter 8

Faculty Days

*In an awakened society,
the best of us would be teachers
and the rest of us would have to
settle for something less.*

LEE IACOCCA

Oberlin was a vanguard school, the first in America to admit Black students and the first to grant bachelor's degrees to women. The college's twenty-nine hundred students were divided between the College of Arts and Sciences and the elite Oberlin Conservatory of Music. This small college town, an intellectual and artistic oasis surrounded by farm country, had a Midwestern charm, especially when autumn burnished the trees with bright colors as the crisp, cool air carried the scents of apples, pumpkins, and spiced tea. It was the first time I would experience four dramatic seasons. I reveled in the first falling snow, my arms open wide as I caught snowflakes on my tongue.

Main Street bordered Tappan Square, a lushly landscaped

park area crisscrossed by walking paths between campus and the town, which had one theater, one supermarket, and one hardware store. I sometimes walked around the Arboretum, a lake and wildlife preserve near a nine-hole public golf course. One of my favorite fellow faculty members was the 1968 Olympic 200-meter champion, Tommie Smith, whose photo (with John Carlos) on the victory stand, his head lowered and a gloved fist raised, had become an iconic image of Black power and peaceful protest.

Chairman Jack (Scott), as I called him due to his revolutionary political leanings and beret with a red star covering a balding head, was a former amateur boxer who retained a trim build and sported a thin mustache. He readily approved all my requests: three trampolines for my new classes, which included "Mirthful Movement," featuring juggling, tumbling, trampoline, tightrope walking, and, as a final exam, an all-class circus performance for the college community. I also coached the men's and women's springboard divers, and both teams would go on to win their conference championships.

Despite a long Ohio winter, the first year passed quickly. After living in a college rental house, Linda and I moved into a faculty resident apartment in one of the college dormitories. My career felt stable, but our distant relationship darkened my days. Linda was at home in a conventional world that repelled me for reasons I couldn't explain. I envied her comfort. I looked at myself in the mirror of our relationship, and I didn't like what I saw. I'd once viewed myself as a knight in shining armor, now tarnished. Even as I played the role of a wise college professor, I felt like a charlatan. *Who am I to teach others when I can't seem to maintain a mature relationship?* I asked myself.

Linda, sensing my discontent, found other, more satisfying relationships, until the weakening thread that held us together finally snapped, and we decided to separate again. What broke my heart was how our daughter Holly, the innocent observer of her parents' growing distance, struggled with each absence.

Meanwhile, I continued wandering in a spiritual wilderness, stumbling toward a light I could barely discern, always flickering in the distance.

Part Two

THE FOUR MENTORS

*We don't receive wisdom;
we must discover it for ourselves
after a journey that no one can
take for us or spare us.*

MARCEL PROUST

I now understand that every human being is on a spiritual quest, but not all of us are aware of it. Who among us does not seek fulfillment, meaning, and an understanding of our place in the universe? The seeds of my own quest, sown in childhood, had by now broken through the soil into the sunlight of conscious awareness, but were not yet ready to bear fruit.

The Indian saint Ramakrishna described the difficulty of trying to open a walnut shell when it was green, but noted how, once it was ripe, it could open with just a tap. All the skills I'd practiced in my youth, and all my experiences, were a part of my ripening process. The first three decades of life prepared me for all that would follow. Now ready to throw myself into any promising possibility, over the next two decades I would meet four radically different mentors who would each offer an initiation for the work to come.

Chapter 9

The Professor

Know thyself.

INSCRIBED ON THE TEMPLE OF APOLLO AT DELPHI

In the spring of my second year at Oberlin, while glancing through a faculty newsletter, I noticed an invitation to apply for a worldwide travel grant to pursue cross-cultural research anywhere in the world. I felt an instant certainty: I was meant to do this. When I was awarded the grant, I had a direction once more, if only for three summer months — another trial separation from Linda and a way to reconnect with a more authentic version of myself as I encountered different cultures around the globe, particularly in Asia, studying mind-body disciplines.

After contacting a few individuals I intended to interview as part of my projected itinerary, I began my journeys to the East by traveling west — to California. Soon after I checked into a hotel, I spoke briefly with Linda and said good night to Holly. Then, on impulse, I called Herb, the former Cal teammate whom I'd consulted prior to my LSD experience. Herb's voice carried a passion and authority as he described a "mind-blowing, life-changing training" he'd recently completed in New York and told me that the next Arica forty-day training would begin in San Francisco in just three days. He recommended that I "drop everything and dive in."

Forty days? I thought — *Why not?* I'd tried many ways to improve myself over the years and enjoyed success in sport and coaching, but the satisfaction never lasted. Having begun to doubt the Western promise of happiness through achievement, I now looked to the Eastern promise involving introspection and inner work, which could lead to self-knowledge, insight, and even a way to transcend the mind. *If I'm going to become a seeker, I might as well go for the mountaintop*, I thought. That's how I ended up in San Francisco in June 1973, in a green-carpeted room on Market Street with seventeen other spiritual seekers.

No Ordinary School

I settled onto one of the *zafu* cushions set up in a large circle. No one chose to take a seat on either side of me, and my fellow students avoided eye contact. That wasn't surprising, since my ears were swollen to grotesque proportions, my eyes nearly shut, and my face and buzz-cut scalp shades of mottled pink and red. I itched everywhere.

A few days earlier I'd gone beach camping with a few friends. Just after dusk, I helped gather brush and twigs for the firepit, unaware that I was holding an armload of poison oak. (I wouldn't have wanted to sit next to me, either.)

Then the work commenced, and I forgot all else. In the coming days, as my rashes disappeared, I found myself immersed, even overwhelmed, by practices and perspectives unlike any I'd experienced before: Arica theory and insight mixed with movement and breathing exercises, including a new form of mind-body calisthenics that opened every major joint and energy center. I practiced mantras and meditations and various challenging exercises from the moment I awoke until I closed my eyes each night, ten to fourteen hours a day.

Our Arica trainers were clean-cut and attractive in a unisex sort of way, with the men clean-shaven and the women's hair relatively short — friendly in an aloof way. Each of them had been trained by the founder of the Arica School. His name was Oscar Ichazo.

Each trainer's duty was to convey information and instructions, reading aloud from the Arica manual and answering relevant questions (since they had more experience with the work). They also listened to some of our small group discussions to help keep us on track. Apart from that, they stayed in the background.

An Origin Story

Coming of age on his father's estate in Bolivia, Oscar had suffered from repeated, paralyzing out-of-body experiences coupled with a premonition of death. Driven by a need to understand his mysterious malady, he devoured books on anatomy, physiology, medicine, and psychology, becoming something of a prodigy. He had inherited his uncle's library, a collection of nearly six hundred books on philosophy and the occult sciences, including fifty volumes of *The Sacred Books of the East*, which he devoured, provoking a desire to learn the practices of these traditions.

Oscar's search led him to a *curandero* and other shamans among the nearby indigenous people. These herbal healers instructed him in plant-based medicines as well as in the proper use of *ayahuasca*, a brew made of plants and vines found in the Amazon. Changing circumstances then led Oscar to intensive, old-world samurai training with Sensei Kentaro Ohara.

He was later invited to Buenos Aires, where he was introduced to a group of advanced spiritual practitioners — elder Sufis and teachers of Kabbalah, alchemy, and Zen. These elders met to share their own cultures' spiritual theories, rituals, and practices. Finding Oscar an adept student, they assigned him different practices so he could report his experiences. They learned much from his reports (as did he) about what sort and combination of exercises were the most effective. After three years of kundalini practice, Oscar finally freed himself from the unpredictable phenomena that had plagued him since childhood.

Oscar would go on to found, in his words, "the root of a new tradition" — a comprehensive mystical school compatible with a modern scientific point of view. He would name the school Arica, after the Chilean city in which he taught. His approach to awakening was based on precise parameters, with the overarching goal of all mystics: unity.

In 1970, a brief but cryptic message arrived at the Esalen Institute, an epicenter of the human potential movement located atop the seaside cliffs of Big Sur, California. The note read: *A fool, filled with love, awaits in the desert.* That desert was the great Atacama, adjacent to the city of Arica, Chile, and the note was signed, *Oscar Ichazo*, a master teacher I'll refer to as the Professor.

Soon after, about fifty Esalen workshop veterans and credentialed professionals, including physician John Lilly and psychiatrist Claudio Naranjo, made a ten-month commitment to travel to Chile to study with the Professor to experience his step-by-step process to enlightenment. On their arrival, Oscar told them, "With full respect for the power of religious faith, a reliance on venerated authorities and unquestioned beliefs can no longer serve modern humanity's evolving needs." In line with an idea attributed to Albert Einstein that we can't solve a problem at the same level of awareness at which it was created, the Professor aimed to lift humanity to a higher level of awareness in order to solve the emerging problems of humanity.

After ten months of intensive study of Arica theory and practice in Chile, the Professor and his core group of teachers relocated to the United States. The movement began, like many things, in New York. When asked about his decision by members of the core group — who'd expected him to begin his public teaching work at Esalen — the Professor replied: "If you can get enlightened in New York City, you can do it anywhere."

An Arica training center also opened in San Francisco, which brings me back to my experiences in the Professor's school.

An Original Teaching

Early in the Arica training the men were asked to shave off facial hair and the women (and some men) to pull back longer hair. A trainer then took our photos, which were mailed to the Professor for his analysis of tension-related asymmetries in each face, associated with neural wiring to the brain. This analysis enabled the Professor to identify each student's *ego-fixation*, one of nine points of sensitivity that indicated unconscious ways of relating to the world.

The notion that facial tension could reveal my (or anyone's) unconscious strategies was totally new to my experience. The nine fixations were depicted via a nine-pointed star within a circle — an enneagram symbol previously used by mystics such as George Gurdjieff. Oscar Ichazo was the first to analyze the structures of the ego in this way for the purpose of self-knowledge. Oscar's seminal work was later adapted and popularized by Helen Palmer and other enneagram authors writing about the fixations primarily as personality types.

In addition to the Professor's map of the structure of the psyche, I also learned, contemplated, discussed, and worked with a new way to "think with the whole body," with each organ answering an essential question, such as "What do I need?" or "What is my capacity?" or "Can (this) be eliminated?" This exercise would later inspire the concept of *body wisdom* in my writing. As our trainer read from the Arica manual, "The body is the projector, the mind is the screen" — an insight derived, in my view, from the Professor's samurai training, because in combat there's no time for rumination. The body must act instantly, instinctively, and decisively.

Despite the cognitive maps and models, the Professor's work was founded on his extensive understanding of the neuroanatomy of the human body. Most of my time in the training was grounded in physical exercises to awaken all organ systems.

My Training and Process

During my time in the Arica training, I was exposed to more than thirty specialized meditation and breathing practices. I also learned so many maps to expand awareness of my psyche, they left my head spinning.

One such map involved the nine primary, often unconscious means that we humans habitually use to compensate for the stresses of life, including alcohol (and other drugs such as tobacco and opiates), psychosomatic illness, hyperactivity, crime, psychic panic, psychoneurosis (or in extreme cases psychosis), overeating, cruelty, and compulsive sexual release. Our class spent an hour each day in small groups, discussing when and where we'd each used one or more of these doors.

The Professor had apparently once said that sex, overeating, and hyperactivity could be used consciously, in a less extreme or dysfunctional manner. He'd added, as an example, "It's better to eat a cookie than to get a headache."

Speaking of eating, we were advised to eat a higher protein

diet with reduced carbs, favoring fish over red meat during the training. Since I didn't eat meat or fish, I used eggs, raw nuts, beans, and dairy protein sources, along with salads and fresh fruit.

Internal Maps and Practices

A significant Arica map dealt with ascending stages of consciousness, beginning with the bottom end of the scale, or *blind belief* — the "opposite of enlightenment," characterized by deep-rooted fear (often masked by bravado), evidenced by tense muscularity, pent-up violence, and a total identification with beliefs disconnected from reality. The trainer explained, "According to Oscar, a large portion of humanity is struggling at this level." I found that statement hard to believe until, decades later, I saw how millions of people still cling to untethered beliefs and conspiracy theories.

The next level, according to our trainer, is *social dogma*, typified by individuals who are locked into conventional and consensus reality, going with the popular fashion of thought, taste, and social agreements, and a concern with what is "proper."

The third level, embodied by certain celebrities, athletes, politicians, rock stars, and criminals, centers around an inflated sense of self as special, superior, and above the rules of law or society.

"Rising to a higher state is possible," said the trainer, "only by seeing through the current level." So once a person moves beyond blind belief, social dogmas, and aggrandized self-image, the psyche clings to self-created mental theories about almost anything.

The next level centers around a dark night of disillusion, where theories no longer suffice and we confront the reality that we are asleep — a realization that opens the way to six higher levels of awareness, culminating in a state of unity that I'd momentarily glimpsed on my LSD journey years before.

Thus, I set out on a path of learning unlike any of my academic or past physical training. We processed these Arica maps with intensive group work, leading to profound but disillusioning self-knowledge. (*Disillusioning* meaning a freeing from illusions, pretense, and self-image.) I had to face the fact that I was still asleep, searching for a way to wake up, which had brought me to the Arica training and propelled me along my path.

Arica offered maps of the territory, but I'd have to make the journey and do the work — intense self-examination accelerated by the group process and supported by the breathwork and meditation practices. In one of these practices I sat facing a partner as we gazed into each other's eyes for five full minutes before moving on to the next partner. The point of this exercise was not personal but transpersonal, connecting each of us to the heart of humanity.

To lighten up after psychologically difficult introspective (shadow) work, we were also introduced to a variety of JERFs, which stands for Joy, Energy, Relaxation, and Fun, including African dance, spirited group chanting, theater games, and partner teamwork exercises that sometimes left us weak with laughter.

In another new meditation, I lay on my back with my hands clasped behind my head and my thumbs pressed against my ears. In the silence that followed, I gradually became aware of ever-deeper layers of internal sound. After that I combined breathwork with slow-motion movements that produced internal heat. Our trainer, reading from the manual, succinctly summarized the multiple benefits of slow, deep breathing, which included "slower heart rate, reduced blood pressure, stimulation of the vagus nerve, which reduces fight-or-flight response, anxiety, and tension."

Another breathing exercise involved a slow inhalation and exhalation timed with the slowly rising and falling refrains of composer Maurice Ravel's *Boléro*. This exercise prepared me for a kundalini practice that opened the spinal channel: I visualized the glowing head of a snake, biting its own tail to form a circle, moving slowly up my spine with each inhalation — I heard and felt a subtle cracking or popping sound — then, after the glowing snake's head rose through the atlas vertebra and curved forward through the hypothalamus and pineal gland, the snake's head traveled down with the exhalation through the front brain, soft palate, throat, heart, and diaphragm, pausing at the perineum, then returning again up the spine. We were told to breathe at our own pace, but for me, each full cycle of inhalation-exhalation took about a minute — sixty breaths or so in the course of an hour. As beads of sweat formed on my forehead, I could understand why this exercise was a part of a training phase called Fire Week.

This work, interspersed with a variety of meditations, mantras, contemplations, visualizations, and breathing practices, was, according to my notes, "like learning to ice-skate blindfolded on top of a speeding vehicle... digging through layers of sediment to find the Mother Lode."

A More Youthful Body

On a Saturday morning, in the warm living room of an old San Francisco Victorian home, I sat in a crowd of mostly naked bodies as two of our trainers taught us, step-by-step, a seven-hour bone-sculpting self-massage that Oscar called *chua ka*, based on a ritual cleansing used by Mongolian warriors to release chronic, fear-based tension. "In this form of bodywork," one of the trainers explained, "each part of the body is associated with a different fear." For example, it took nearly a full hour just to process the feet, said to hold the "fear of being oneself."

"Why are the feet associated with this particular fear?" I asked.

"The whole body is represented in the feet," she answered. "And tension there prevents a conscious connection to the earth."

The aim was to smooth out bumps or, as they called them, "globules of fear" on every bone surface, first using my hands, then with a wooden *ka*, a tool used to dig deeper.

One of the trainers explained that according to the Professor, this self-massage is a way of "taking direct responsibility for your own evolution." In a sense, this *chua ka* process reflected the essence of the entire training, demonstrating the psychophysical work necessary to prepare body and mind for awakening, similar to how we might clean and organize our home for a special guest.

When I finished the process, my body felt as relaxed and lithe as a young child's. Over the passing months, I'd repeat this self-massage numerous times with cumulative results. I had to remind myself that the purpose of this bone massage was not "letting go of fear," but instead releasing chronic, fear-based tensions I'd accumulated over the years.

Rebirth of the Senses

Near the end of the Arica training, as instructed, I found an empty room for the weekend, in my case at the Berkeley Y. I cleared the room of furniture except for a mattress on the floor, covered the window with a sheet to dim the light and eliminate any distracting view. I brought just enough food to sustain me along with a gallon jug of water. No books or other forms of diversion were allowed. For trips to the bathroom, I was told to keep my eyes half closed and to avoid interacting with other people if at all possible.

I entered the room on Friday evening and departed on Monday morning. During that long weekend, I found the solitude peaceful, boring, and at times maddening. I sat, paced, and sat some more. Other than light stretching, I was to do no exercise, meditation, or masturbation — just me and my so-called mind as the hours ticked by.

On Monday morning I stepped outside into a sunlit day, overwhelmed by a sensory feast: the blue depth of the sky, the blend of traffic sounds and guitar music, laughter and conversation. I plucked a leaf and smelled its aroma, delighting in the world with the fresh senses of a child.

I thought about how infants exist in a sensory Garden of Eden where everything is fresh. Our fall from grace begins as names and concepts obscure direct perception, and we begin to see the world through a veil of associations, beliefs, and interpretations — the memories of things more than the thing itself. *Maybe*, I thought, *I can find satisfaction not by seeking more, but by developing a capacity to appreciate less.*

An hour later, back in San Francisco in that carpeted room I knew so well, I completed the last day of the Arica training at an evening celebration, filled with expressions of gratitude to our trainers and to Oscar Ichazo, the Professor I had encountered only through his extraordinary school.

World Travel: Search and Research

After the Arica training, I felt like a citizen of the cosmos. Flush with a new understanding of myself and the human condition, I finally set out on my overseas travels. My open ticket on Pan American World Airways meant that I could travel to nearly any major city they serviced around the globe without prebooking any flights. My itinerary included California, then Hawaii, Japan, Okinawa, Hong Kong, India, Greece, and a brief overnight on the coast of Portugal before flying to New York, then back to Ohio. Other than contacting a few key people prior to my departure, my schedule and plans were wide open.

Traveling light, with only a small backpack, I flew from San Francisco to Los Angeles. After a heart-tugging phone call to

Holly and a brief visit with my parents, I joined a practice session at a local aikido dojo, blending, flowing, falling, and rolling.

Later, I visited Gordon Doversola, my former Okinawa-te sensei, who helped me relearn the 108-move Falling Leaf *kata* — a routine I'd learned in high school.

At the California Institute of the Arts, I interviewed tai chi master Marshall Ho'o and learned the Cosmic Stance, a standing energy meditation I'd later teach to my Oberlin students. Just after that class, in one of many synchronicities during my travels, I was surprised to run into author Carlos Castaneda. Since I'd read his first two books and found them fascinating, I attended his brief talk at Cal Arts that afternoon. Although he insisted that his books were "true accounts," I had my doubts. Literally true or not, his evocative writing had intrigued a legion of readers.

Driving north, I stopped by Esalen, where I attended a seminar on the Gestalt psychology of Fritz Perls, then participated in a two-day Enlightenment Intensive centered on a koanlike partner contemplation, "Tell me who you are," which eventually generated a (mindless) satori state that lasted for several hours. It felt, for a time, like I was back in the Arica training.

Soon after landing in Oahu, Hawaii, I met with Dr. Lily Siou, head of the Six Chinese Arts School for *chi kung*, blending elements of breathing, concentration, and slow movement in line with Chinese Five Elements theory to open meridians where *chi* is said to circulate. I also found a few hours of pure fun with friends in the Waikiki Acrobatic Troupe, doing handstands and tumbling on a lush lawn between the zoo and the beach, with a sea breeze carrying the sweet aroma of 'ilima blossoms.

At sunrise on the day of my departure, I entered a high school gym for a seminar with Koichi Tohei-sensei, a leading aikido master who demonstrated the power of *ki* (also called *chi* or *prana*) in an Unbendable Arm exercise I'd learned in my early aikido days, which shows how a relatively relaxed arm can easily remain extended as a partner applies increasing pressure to bend it. Formerly an asthmatic child, Tohei had developed impressive breath control, which he demonstrated by taking a deep breath, then exhaling continuously into a microphone for a full minute before emitting a loud martial arts shout (or *kiai*) with his remaining air — a perfect send-off to Japan.

After I landed at Narita Airport, the change of environments and time zones generated a dreamlike experience: an elderly Japanese Samaritan who left his train to show me the way to a small hostel near Shinjuku Station in Tokyo ... the kimono-clad woman who bowed, then directed me to remove my sandals and wash my feet on that warm night, handing me a small towel and a set of indoor slippers ... entering the foyer to meet an American martial arts teacher named Bill Thomas, a sturdy-looking fellow who volunteered to be my tour guide.

In the city of Kyoto, we made an all-night pilgrimage up Mount Fuji to view sunrise from the peak. The seven-hour upward hike was followed by a satisfying sprint down the granulated lava-covered mountain, shredding my sneakers in the process.

For the rest of my travels that hot summer, I wore wooden *geta* sandals and carried a Fuji-san walking stick. Despite their strange appearance, I found the *geta* comfortable, and the walking stick, which was allowed on airplanes, encouraged me to walk at a calm and measured pace. After the Arica training (my version of a Shaolin temple), I felt like the *Kung Fu* character Kwai Chang Caine, a lone traveler on a quest.

The next day, Bill and I visited the Kodokan, center of judo (gentle way); the Hombu-dojo, world headquarters of aikido; and the Japan Karate Association, where I observed a training session just before I caught my next flight.

I spent one quiet but memorable evening in Okinawa: After finding an unlocked and empty dojo late in the evening, I removed my shoes and performed the Falling Leaf form, then sat a while in meditation. Back at the tiny airport, I washed up in the restroom on the second floor, snuck out an open window overlooking the concrete overhang, laid out my bedroll, and fell asleep under a starry sky.

At dawn, I washed away the night's sweat and caught a flight to Hong Kong, where I stayed two sweltering nights in a seedy hotel whose air-conditioning consisted of a rattling overhead fan. The next morning, before catching my flight to Calcutta, India, I practiced tai chi at sunrise with Chinese elders in a park.

My flight to Calcutta arrived at dusk. Since I hadn't prebooked any housing, I trusted a taxi driver to find me a hostel, which turned out to be a bare room no larger than a walk-in closet. I finally drifted to sleep, awakened periodically by rats scampering beneath my raised, straw-filled sleeping pallet. The next morning, assailed by smells of sweat and dung mixed with various spices for sale, I explored an open-air market, purchasing a few postcards, a souvenir for Linda, and a trinket for Holly.

Madras, in Southern India, was a short distance from Pondicherry and the ashram of the late Sri Aurobindo, a renaissance man straddling the worlds of poetry, political action, and Integral Yoga. Just outside his utopian city of Auroville, I met Norman Dowsett, the busy ashram manager, who explained that they couldn't spare anyone to show me around due to a big festival later that day. About to depart, I noticed a few photos under glass, one of which showed a gymnast swinging around the high bar. When I mentioned that I had gymnastics experience, Mr. Dowsett told me that their local gymnastics instructor was ill, and asked if I might perform on the horizontal bar for the village children.

After my high bar routine, which seemed to delight the children, I was given a tour of Auroville after all.

In Bombay (now Mumbai), I visited Sri Yogendra, a white-bearded yogi who shook his finger at attendees to make his points. Head of the Scientific Yoga Institute, he spoke of the many levels of yogic art and science.

During a short visit to Athens, Greece, surrounded by other tourists at the Parthenon, I communed with the spirits of the ancient philosophers before my flight home. Then, after a one-night layover in Cascais, Portugal, I caught a trans-Atlantic flight to New York City.

As I drifted off to sleep on the long flight, an array of images floated through my memory like cloud reveries: hot mineral baths and sea spray from waves crashing against the cliffs of Big Sur and the cawing of gulls in the dawn-lit sky...rainbow fireworks bursting over the Waikiki surf while eating ravioli on a friend's houseboat...a pink sunrise seen from the peak of Mount Fuji in the chilled air at twelve thousand feet...Japanese children playing with five-inch-long pet bugs...getting scrubbed squeaky clean in a Japanese hot bath...running my hand across the lichen and moss near a Zen pond in the spare silence of a rock garden. Everywhere, people going about their lives, earning a living and, perhaps like me, seeking meaning and purpose, love and understanding.

In reflection, my world travels only served as a postscript to the transformation I experienced in the Arica training. I'd flown around the globe, searching for the mystical East only to discover that the East was away visiting San Francisco.

Homecoming

Linda and Holly were waiting for me when I got off the plane in Ohio. Holly ran to me, squealing with delight, and hugged me tight. My embrace with Linda was warm but empty of real intimacy, like hugging an old friend. It was now obvious that time and experience had drawn us in different directions. Linda had not been lonely (or alone) in my absence, which I understood.

I was struck by the stark divide between the Arica training exercises and the realities of everyday life in the real world. After all the intensive work, my breath control and concentration had improved and my body felt more open, but little else had really changed. All those meditations and other practices were no more helpful in my everyday life than my ability to do an iron cross or a twisting somersault. I was more self-aware but still self-absorbed, more open to observing myself objectively but still plagued by my failing marriage. At least I was now willing to face the fact that we were married in name only. We just hadn't found a reason or impetus to divorce.

A Sense of Joy

Then, that autumn of 1973, something small and great and wonderful appeared out of nowhere. I met a woman named Joyce, who was beginning her final year at Oberlin. I was then twenty-seven years old; she was twenty-one. When Joyce knocked on our door and entered our dorm apartment to do some ironing for Linda, a puff of magic entered with her, and the world, the moment, was no longer ordinary. Her short black hair hung in bangs above large dark eyes and a bright smile.

I'd been listening to a new Cat Stevens album, so I offered her the headphones while she ironed. We spoke only briefly that evening but, like that old service station mechanic years earlier, she left a strong impression. Without having any idea what role she would play in my life, I felt a sense of recognition, as if we'd met before. It reminded me of something guitar maestro Andrés Segovia once said of the first time he ever picked up the instrument and began to play: "It didn't feel like learning; it felt like remembering."

By this time, Linda and I were essentially living separate lives with our own interests, values, and friends, parenthood our only common ground. We lived together for Holly, and for the sake of convenience.

Since Joyce lived in the dorm, I'd sometimes see her in the lobby, and once at the Rathskeller café on campus, where she worked a few hours a day. I told her a few things about the forty-day Arica training. Realizing that words fell short, I asked if she might like to try a meditation that involved gazing into each other's eyes — a provocative suggestion for a married man to make, but my motives in that moment were well-intentioned. Joyce seemed intrigued with my descriptions of the Arica training and with the meditation, and maybe a little intrigued with me.

After class, while we walked around the Arboretum and past the small golf course, Joyce told me a story about the day of her birth: When her mother told the nurse that her baby's name was Joy, the nurse misheard and wrote Joyce on the birth certificate. Her mother, who came from a different era, believed she had to accept what was written on the legal document, so the name stuck. Joyce confided that she'd always wanted to use the name her mother had intended, which she preferred. So from then on, she became Joy.

During the month of January, Oberlin students were allowed to pursue an area of independent study on campus or anywhere else. I suggested that Joy look into an upcoming Arica training in Atlanta beginning just after New Year's Day 1974. After some research, she decided to enroll.

Joy's Memories

Here is how I remember meeting Dan: His wife Linda had hired me to do childcare and some ironing for her. Like most college students, I needed the money, and she paid extra well for ironing — fifteen dollars an hour! While I was ironing Dan's sweatshirt (who irons sweatshirts?), I heard his voice before I saw him. He said something like, "While you're working, check out this music," handing me wired headphones connected to a nearby stereo. I remember liking the music but feeling a bit disoriented by the experience — I wanted to hear Dan's voice more than the music.

A few weeks later I recall sitting in my dorm room, looking out the window and thinking about Dan. It felt as if we somehow knew each other. I even remember speaking aloud to myself, "It's like I've known him for twenty years" (which, at age twenty-one, was ridiculous).

Since my dorm room was across the hall from Dan and Linda's apartment, we all saw one another frequently. At that time I knew Linda better than I knew Dan. Holly and I had a good relationship from the start.

On a whim, I signed up for Dan's beginning gymnastics class. Unlike the instructors of other PE classes I'd taken at Oberlin, Dan broke down each skill into easy parts, and clearly explained each step. Later that semester, I commented to a friend on campus, "This guy could teach anything."

We sometimes spoke after class. He told me about the Arica forty-day training. At that time I felt directionless, having changed my major several times. Now a senior,

I decided to do the Arica training, which meant going to Atlanta during Oberlin's four-week winter break, and returning to Oberlin two weeks into my final semester. After I submitted a proposal, the registrar's office allowed this absence and even gave me ten college credits for the course.

Advanced Work

After Joy left for the winter holidays and her Arica training, I flew to New York City for a two-week advanced training designed to "further clarify consciousness to the point of illumination." It would also prepare any interested graduate to become an Arica trainer in one of the centers opening around the United States and overseas.

My desire to understand myself and other people had begun in my early teenage years as I tried to grasp why my older sister (and by extension, other people) behaved in unpredictable ways. That urge to understand had prompted my choice of psychology as a major, but most college courses had left me unsatisfied. Only now had I found the clarity I'd sought.

If the Arica forty-day training had been the first stage of a multistage rocket breaking free of Earth's gravity, this second stage catapulted me into inner space, along with about two hundred other Aricans, as we now called ourselves.

The Professor's advanced training highlighted "the nine domains of consciousness": sentiments, life and security, creativity, intellectual, social, work, hierarchies, conduct and morals, and spiritual domains. My fellow students and I walked around Manhattan, identifying each domain in which we found ourselves; for example, pet stores (sentiments), jewelers (hierarchies), bookstores and libraries (intellectual), bars and cafés (social; life and security), and police stations (life and security; conduct and morals). More important, this work also illuminated the human psyche, since thoughts, opinions, and judgments fell into one of the nine domains.

The work then revealed two polarized characters within each domain. For example, I learned that in the domain of sentiments, each human psyche contains both a rigid character and a softer, sentimental side. And in the conduct and morals domain, we each possess (and are in a sense possessed by) a hedonistic, self-indulgent character and, at the opposite pole, a puritanical, self-denying side. These opposing characters create internal contradiction, like the proverbial devil on one shoulder and angel on the other. I saw how I might behave more like one character while internally feeling like the other — for example, acting out a hedonist tendency while my inner puritan criticized such self-indulgence.

I got to know and accept all these characters through partner theater exercises, finding clarity and balance rather than unconsciously acting out one side while internally struggling with the other. This work to clarify consciousness, much like meditation, provided distance from each of the characters, so I became less identified with either side and was able to treat life as theater, with less attachment to one or another character as being innately true or superior. I came to view each of these characters, in myself and in others, with humor and compassion. In other words, I could no longer take myself so seriously, or be as judgmental about the characters that animated other people.

I also learned that the way I viewed myself could be quite different from the way others perceived me. Surrounded by two hundred participants at the advanced training, I assumed that I was anonymous — all but invisible. Apparently, I was mistaken. Months later, I learned that a few trainers had referred to me as "the robot" due to my serious and stoical disposition. While I thought I was simply being an earnest, rigorous trainee, striving to do all the exercises properly, and give it my best effort (as was my habit from gymnastics), I apparently stood out among other, more casual aspirants.

My efforts, however, hadn't generated any noticeable outcomes until, abruptly, a rather odd awakening occurred.

Kensho

During the second week of the advanced training, while practicing the Arica calisthenics routine, I continued repeating an internal mantra as we'd been instructed to do throughout the day: "Everything is my dream… everything is my dream… everything is my dream —"

In the next moment, out of nowhere, I experienced a *kensho* — a sudden insight that everything *was* my dream! It hit me like a slap, and I exploded with laughter! It was as if I'd just gotten the punchline to a cosmic joke. All those years of interpreting meanings, and worrying about whether people liked me, was all my own creation! *Now, how could any of that possibly matter ever again?*

Nothing changed, yet everything changed. Life, this moment, *all* of it, was my dream, my creation, my illusion. In truth everything arose simply as it was. The beliefs, projections, opinions, and complications "I" had imposed upon reality fell away. What remained was a mysterious, spontaneous moment-to-moment experiencing, an obvious truth that had escaped my notice. In those few untroubled moments of free attention, the mind constructs and noise fell away. *How could I have missed it?* I thought.

I also wondered whether this was the illumination Oscar had promised. I shared what had occurred with one of the trainers;

he seemed to shrug it off or didn't know what to say. None of the other students I spoke with reported a similar experience. I stopped speaking of it because words couldn't do it justice.

Meeting the Professor

A few days before the advanced training ended, I learned that the Professor himself was scheduled to give a talk that evening. It would be the first and only time I'd ever see him in person. Oscar had deliberately remained at the periphery because the work wasn't about him. (I could get an education without meeting the headmaster.) Still, the stories of his training with masters of many spiritual traditions elevated him to iconic status in my mind. *What kind of a person could have developed such an amazing body of work?* I wondered.

I was one of the first to arrive outside the training facility on West 57th Street in Manhattan, two blocks south of Central Park. A crowd of students quickly formed, hugging themselves against the chill air, waiting for the doors to open. A thrill of anticipation ran up my spine on that December evening as the crowd parted like the Red Sea to let the Professor walk through the door. I could see that he was neither tall nor short, just a slim, relaxed man in his early forties, who walked with the grace of a cat.

It turned out the door was locked. Oscar asked if anyone had a key. In those few pregnant moments, he seemed surrounded by light — no doubt a trick of the streetlights.

Soon after, we all streamed in to find a good seat on one of hundreds of meditation cushions on the plush, green-carpeted floor. In the softly lit room, I noted the Professor's thinning dark hair cut short, a lean, angular face, a thin mustache, and dark eyes that seemed to reveal both power and compassion. Or maybe it was just my own projection.

Oscar gave a brief talk about the Arica School, then mentioned that he was working on a complete history of the world's spiritual traditions. Then he asked for questions, of which I can only recall a few. Someone asked about the cause of cancer. Oscar said something to the effect that the body has cancerous cells that are normally neutralized by the immune system, until a combination of genetics, diet, and environmental pollution drives the body out of the natural pattern.

Someone else asked whether humans might one day travel to other planets and star systems. The Professor remarked that long-distance space travel faced the challenge of "ionizing radiation," and explained how a low-gravity environment affected the bones and entire physiology.

In response to a question about hidden teachings contained in Greek mythology, Oscar offered the example of the Gorgon Medusa, a winged figure who had writhing, venomous snakes in place of hair. According to myth, anyone who gazed upon her would turn to stone. He explained that the snakes coming out of her head represented the constant stream of random, discursive thoughts he referred to as *chicharrero* (abbreviated as *chich*), a word referring to the incessant chirping of the cicada, mental chatter that can distract or even paralyze someone from effective action.

In my only personal exchange with the Professor, I asked, "Oscar, you've spoken of working the *bardo*, the space between lives. According to this theory of reincarnation, with the world population expanding so rapidly, how are new souls created for the millions of babies born?" He responded with an analogy about "a great tree growing new limbs and bearing more fruit."

The Professor closed the training with a bow and a long *om* salutation. Then he walked out of the room. It was the last time I would personally see Oscar Ichazo, but somehow once was enough.

Joy's Memories

Arica was unlike anything I'd ever done. My group was small — consisting of nine people, including a fellow Oberlin student with whom I shared a room. I was in a daze for most of the experience. I did all the bodywork and breathwork and studied the Arica theory, but I can't say it made sense to me in the same way it did for Dan. Prior to the Arica training, I hadn't read books about spiritual practice or studied anything but conventional college courses. But when it was over, I did feel differently about my world. Now my ordinary issues felt secondary to the bigger picture of life.

When I returned to Oberlin in mid-February, my relationship with Dan had also changed. We now shared an understanding and language, and we related not as student and professor, but as equals — as Aricans. Dan and I never lacked things to talk about before Arica, but now our conversations took on a new depth, and anything seemed possible.

Dan's relationship with Linda was complicated from my view. When I first saw them together, they seemed like an ordinary, happy couple. But on my return, I noticed their distance from each other. Linda spent much of her time talking with students or doing her own thing. Dan was busy teaching but also seemed to have more free time on his own than a married person would usually have. Dan and Linda never really fought or displayed much in the way of drama between them. If anything, that's what surprised people who knew them as a couple, and why it wasn't obvious their relationship was troubled. I suppose they were just a mismatch.

All of this felt awkward since I had no intention of causing problems. I was twenty-two years old, Dan was now twenty-eight, and Linda was twenty-six — all of us young and naïve, and everyone, it seemed, caught up in the ethos of the 1970s, breaking loose from previously accepted conventions. There were no college rules at that time forbidding relationships between students and faculty. And since Linda spent time with other people, I didn't feel bad about spending time with Dan. In fact, it felt completely right. I was attracted to Dan and he to me. Linda, involved in other relationships, seemed oblivious or didn't care.

In my last semester at Oberlin, on the first day of spring, Dan served as my guide when I dropped acid. (I'd had more experiences with alcohol and marijuana than Dan, but I wasn't a regular user.) I'd prepared for this LSD trip by reading several books about the experience. It was a revelatory journey I never felt the need to repeat but was glad that I had experienced.

Learn One Day, Teach One Day

When I returned to Oberlin from the advanced training, the intensity of my *kensho* experience and other new insights faded over the passing weeks, like coming down from an LSD experience, dissolving into memory impressions.

Still, fueled by fresh insights, I designed several new Oberlin courses, the first of which I titled Psychophysical Development, featuring basic elements from the Arica training that I had understood and embodied. It was a sample menu; only the Arica School could provide the full meal. The second course featured the internal martial arts of aikido and tai chi. I first chose the title Way of the Warrior, but that didn't quite fit, so I changed it to Way of the *Peaceful* Warrior. Both new courses were soon filled to capacity.

Then spring came, bringing its own changes. After Joy graduated from Oberlin, she returned to her parents' home in New Jersey. Soon after, I hitchhiked to Los Angeles to visit my parents for a few weeks.

When I returned to Oberlin, I took care of Holly for the rest of the summer while Linda, entirely of her own accord, enrolled in the Arica forty-day training in Colorado to broaden her experience. She returned to Oberlin at summer's end, in a temporary narrowing of the rift between us.

I didn't know whether I'd ever see Joy again.

Another Step toward Enlightenment?

In the autumn of 1974, the Professor created a third level of training that he named Opening the Rainbow Eye. The training workbook opened with these words: "When consciousness is recognized as permanent and unchanging, it is said that the internal witness is awake."

I immersed myself in this work each evening. In one of many complex meditations, I gazed at a sequence of pages, each showing a precise color that I inhaled, as instructed, into a major organ system until I could visualize and sense each organ glowing with that color and its associated quality, an approach quite different from an academic study of anatomy. I felt somehow more together and complete as awareness pulsed through every organ with each breath and heartbeat.

Newly inspired, I learned of the planned opening of an Arica teaching house in Berkeley, California, and I asked Linda whether, for this reason, she might like to return to the Bay Area. Even though our marriage was on life support by that time, each move, every change of scene and circumstance, seemed to reinvigorate our relationship for a short time. So, when she agreed to the move, I notified the dean of the College of Arts and Sciences of my intention to leave at the end of the term and teach in "a different sort of school."

The Method That Wasn't

After our return to Berkeley and with Holly now in kindergarten, Linda found work in downtown Berkeley and I threw myself into helping transform an old warehouse space into the new Arica center with coats of paint, an orange-and-white parachute canopy, and plush carpet.

Then the Professor announced a new public outreach for the Arica School he called "The Method of Expansion," beginning with a new weekend program.

Like many visionaries, Oscar was ahead of his time. Those who looked to the East and practiced inner work remained a relatively small group of outliers (in contrast, say, to the millions of yoga devotees today). So the Professor's promised expansion imploded instead. Within a few months, the Berkeley teaching center closed its doors. Other closings would follow. Given the depth of the Professor's knowledge and the quality of the Arica work, I found this change profoundly disappointing and also puzzling. But, as my experience coaching at Stanford revealed, merit alone is not always rewarded.

In the weeks that followed, I began writing a series of articles for *International Gymnast Magazine* about broader principles for effective learning and living, corresponding to my expanding perspectives. As the stack of articles grew into a thick pile resembling a manuscript, it struck me for the first time: *I might even write a book someday.*

Reflections on the School

The Professor was not selling success, power, healing, wealth, past-life access, or how to communicate with the other side. Instead, Arica required (and developed) a person's willingness to dissect their own psyche. Oscar's aim was illumination, not high achievement. Yet even for fully engaged students, the promise of enlightenment waited at the top of an ascending staircase at the far end of the rainbow.

Around this time the Professor announced a fourth level of work. Rumors circulated that there would eventually be a fifth, sixth, seventh, eighth, and possibly a ninth level, leading finally to the promised enlightenment. This news brought to mind Charlie Brown, the *Peanuts* comic strip character, who would repeatedly attempt to kick a football held by Lucy. Every time he kicked, Lucy would pull the ball away at the last second and Charlie would end up on his back, emitting a sigh. Lucy promised that she'd leave the ball in place next time, but she continued pulling the ball away. *Is there a message here?* I asked myself. *When will Charlie say, "Enough"? When will I?*

Years before, Coach Frey explained the principle of *specificity* — that is, one gets better at running by running, and better at somersaults by somersaulting. In Arica, the breathing exercises, meditations, visualizations, and chanting helped me get better at doing inner work. These exercises also contributed to a more balanced body and enhanced self-awareness. But the Arica work in itself could not clarify my career directions or heal an ailing marriage. Doubt and a disillusion overshadowed my initial belief in the Arica School. As the old proverb goes, "Before enlightenment, chopping wood and carrying water. After enlightenment, chopping wood and carrying water." And after all my training, I remained a self-absorbed and assertively independent guy. At least Arica had helped me to face this fact. Maybe it also afforded me the space to make a change.

So, with appreciation for all that the Professor had created, I decided to end my formal connection. Having made this decision and stepped off the merry-go-round, I could recommit to everyday life. But what would that life look like? What life did I truly want to live?

Coincident with the dissolution of the Berkeley Arica Center, our marriage also finally ended. It was as amicable as it was inevitable. I signed the papers, then helped Linda and Holly move into a house in Berkeley. I understood my reasons for getting married and now divorced. The only mystery was why we'd persisted for nearly eight years.

Now on my own, I found part-time work teaching an adult martial arts and acrobatics course at the Berkeley Y.

Bardo: The Space between Lives

After relying on fortune's favor through my early years, the bottom had dropped out. Now single, unemployed, and unmoored, I was suffering from decision fatigue. With ruminations leading nowhere, I visited a Navy recruiting office and took an exam, thinking that officer candidate school might at least afford some structure — maybe even a disciplined, organized career. I did well on the exam, but they told me that twenty-nine years old was past their cutoff for officer training. It was the first time I'd ever been too old for anything.

Once again feeling like a ghost, I was forced to take stock of my life and circumstance and the role I'd played in it. As I reflected on my youthful gymnastics and college years, and the night I'd met that old service station attendant and what he inspired, I wondered: *What would Socrates say?*

A Dialogue with Socrates

On New Year's Day 2021, as I was completing the seventh draft of this book, the face of Socrates appeared in my mind's eye. I heard him clear his throat — a good trick since he was incorporeal.

"Where the hell did you come from, Soc? And where have you been?"

Big questions. Let's just say I was never far away.

"But aren't you dead by now or...in the light or — oh, never mind."

Never mind? That's a positive sign.

"Maybe, but I'm still not enlightened."

Who gives a shit?

"I did have some glimpses, but it didn't last. Never does."

Nice observation.

"Wow, an actual compliment. I —"

So what have you been up to, Dan?

"You should know that if you're in my head —"

Look a little lower in the body.

"Okay then — in my heart."

Let's not get sappy.

"So you're my muse, right?"

Have been all along.

"Well then, Mr. Know-It-All, what do you think of my training with the Professor?"

How about I ask the questions and you give the answers, Junior?

"Stop with the Junior stuff, will you? I'm seventy-five freakin' years old!"

Consider my age…

"Point taken — guess I'll always be Junior to you."

What do you really think about your training in that Arica School?

"I already wrote about it —"

Come on, spill it!

"Well, I learned a lot about myself."

What self?

"Don't go all Zen on me, Socrates! You know very well that I'm referring to my psyche — the ego structures and strategies. The Professor's work opened new perspectives, new ways of looking at myself and the world. Expanded awareness — a lot that was unconscious is more conscious now. And my body never felt better. Although none of it helped my marriage to Linda."

Or, apparently, your maturity. Anyway, what you just told me sounds like brochure copy.

"My point is that there was a firewall between all that inner work in Arica and the actual stuff of daily life. Meanwhile, I kept hoping that the work would lead me to a final awakening."

In the conventional world, enlightenment and ten bucks will get you a short taxi ride.

"Exactly. Spiritual awakening doesn't do the laundry, wash the dishes, or get the shopping done."

And no separate self can attain it since illumination dissolves that illusory sense of separation. In other words, there's no I in enlightenment.

"Well, technically, there is a small *i*, but we agree on the larger point: Awakened beings, being human, will still face the difficulties of life in relationships, finances, health — that sort of thing. I'm just thinking aloud, here —"

It's called 'talking.'

"You're as witty as ever, but let me finish. On the plus side, those enlightened moments I've experienced seemed to catapult me to a transcendent perspective, embracing all that arises, even though practical challenges remain — I still have to function in everyday life. Wasn't it Ram Dass who said, 'We can be lost in cosmic bliss but still be responsible for remembering our postal code'?"

A wise fellow, that Ram Dass.

"And while we're on the topic, since we agree that enlightenment is not a practical goal, why did you inspire me to write in *Way of the Peaceful Warrior* about passing through the gate?"

That's what seemed to interest you at the time.

"You know, Socrates, you seem to have changed."

So have you, Dan — not a coincidence, I think.

"So how does this go? Do I say something, then wait for your response? I'm kind of new at this."

We've been working together all along — how do you think you wrote all those books?

"Oh, so now you're taking credit? This is so weird."

Life is weird. Speaking of which, would you care to share any summary impressions from all your Arica work?

"Well, here's the thing: It was brilliant the way the practices and maps built upon each other. I really can't imagine a more comprehensive school, but —"

But?

"There's something I can't quite —"

Face?

"Yeah, maybe that's it. Maybe I'm not ready to face or see that it didn't change my everyday life."

You spent half your time analyzing your craziness and the other half dramatizing it.

"You still have a way with words, Soc. But there's something else: The Arica training was a spiritual boot camp — like a gymnastics camp for the soul. I took home specialized skills and insights, but the inner work only helped me get better at inner work. It didn't help me balance a checkbook, find a career, or repair a broken relationship. But maybe I did learn one useful thing: To improve my daily life —"

You have to practice daily life.

"Do you have to finish my sentences like that? It gets a bit irritating —"

It seems like you've learned something after all.

"Maybe so. But I wonder whether the Professor understood all of that. Or maybe he was too caught up in his system and school."

I expect that he meant well. After all, he dedicated his life to this school, his legacy.

"I'm grateful to Oscar and to the Arica School, but I have no impulse to continue — it's just not for me."

Like when you'd go into a bookstore and skip over some book —

"Yes! Because I'd been there, done that —"

And you passed over others because you weren't ready yet.

"That too."

But when you found the right book for you, at just the right time: magic.

"Like finding a gold nugget."

And after you finish a book?

"I either keep it on my shelf or give it away."

But some ideas become a part of you, like the Arica work. It was yours only for a time, but the perspectives remain, sitting on your shelf —

"Socrates! Are you referring to shelf realization?"

Hmm...I think we're done, for now.

"Feels like it. And thanks for...Soc?"

His presence vanished as quickly as it had appeared. He had a way of doing that.

Chapter 10

The Guru

*There are no bridges between
the real world and mystical world
so we must make a leap of faith.*

Søren Kierkegaard

I'd come of age in a time of transformation. After the idealism of the psychedelic "Make love not war" 1960s, I surfed waves of change through the soul-searching 1970s and the New Age movement with its array of Eastern teachers, gurus, schools, and spiritual seekers eager to explore, experiment, and test the boundaries of reality. *Everything* was on the table. What followed can best be understood as a reflection of these changing times.

Just before my thirtieth birthday, in the face of these emerging values, feeling untethered and directionless, I came upon an oddly titled memoir, *The Knee of Listening*, written by an American spiritual teacher in his thirties named Franklin Jones, whom I'll refer to as the Guru. He wore no beard, beads, or robe. He'd studied philosophy at Columbia University, then earned an MA in English from Stanford.

After Jones wrote his first book, then a second, he began to attract followers. But in contrast to the Professor's evolving teaching, the Guru's method involved no effortful techniques but rather a direct, openhearted communion with a Divine Reality that was, in his words, "always, already the case." And while the Professor had remained in the background, the Guru's physical form and spiritual presence lay at the epicenter of a growing community of devotees as a direct means of transcendence.

One Light, Many Lamps

Given all that had come before, I was naturally drawn to the extraordinary insights, humor, and creativity of this homespun American master. When someone asked him to comment on Oscar Ichazo's claim that the Arica School "required no beliefs," the Guru laughed aloud and said, "Of course that school requires beliefs; you have to believe it's going to do something for you!" He soon followed up with: "I'd rather beat you with a stick than tell you to meditate your way to enlightenment." When he described his sense of enlightenment as "alternating at the speed of light between the heights of ecstasy and depths of despair" I could somehow relate to his unique perspective.

I'd not yet seen Franklin Jones in person, but the numinous sensation I felt while reading his work was probably similar to the feelings of Christians reading the New Testament, Muslims reading the Koran, or Jews reading the Talmud. Returning again and again to his words, I found a sense of spiritual nourishment that lifted me above the troubles of this world.

I wasn't alone in my views. Alan Watts, a respected scholar and author on Zen and Taoism, wrote, "Although I do not know Franklin Jones personally, what he says, and says very well, is something that I have been trying to express for thirty-five years."

Ken Wilber, another noted author and scholar, wrote elsewhere, "I've put forward five books and thirty-odd articles devoted to a synthesis of Eastern and Western religion and psychology.... And my opinion is that we have, in the person of [the Guru], a Spiritual Master and religious genius of the ultimate degree ... [and his teachings] are discussed with such brilliance that one can only conclude that he understands them better than their originators."

By his own admission, Franklin Jones was not some goody-goody, celibate, white-clad holy man. In an essay titled "The Man of Understanding," from the 1973 edition of his first book, he forewarned readers and foreshadowed all that would follow when he wrote:

> The man of understanding is not entranced. He is not elsewhere. He is not having an experience. He is awake. He is present.... He may seem to be addicted to every kind of foolishness and error. How could it be otherwise? There is only the ordinary. He is not spiritual. He is not religious. He is not philosophical. He is not moral. He is not fastidious, lean and lawful.... He appears as every kind of persuasion.... His living coaxes everyone only to understand.... He is a seducer, a madman, a hoax, a libertine, a fool.... He demonstrates the futility of all things.... Therefore he makes understanding the only possibility. And understanding makes no difference at all. Except it is reality, which was already the case.

I never took these words literally, but as poetic prose to convey that he was not, in his words, "some pipe-smoking philosopher." He forewarned followers that he would assert what we denied and deny what we asserted; that is, whatever best served this great process of awakening. From the beginning, the Guru aligned his work with the crazy-wisdom tradition, which seemed to give notice that he was an unconventional teacher. That was fine with me; I'd had enough of conventional ones.

I called the Dawn Horse Bookstore on Polk Street in San Francisco (just a mile from the Arica forty-day training site) and arranged to attend an orientation to the Guru's community.

The Conditions for Being Human

I entered the community bookstore a few evenings later, inhaling the faint aroma of incense as I surveyed an assortment of books from various spiritual traditions, with the Guru's first three books prominently displayed. His photo hung on the wall, revealing the bright, clear-eyed self-assurance and energy of a man in his early thirties with a full head of hair, dark and heavy brows, and a mouth poised to smile or laugh.

In the carpeted meeting room, just after I sat down among ten or twelve people, a man and woman in their forties stood behind a lectern, welcomed us, introduced themselves, and said a few words about their initiation into the community. They then announced that Franklin Jones had taken the new name of Bubba Free John to mark a new phase of his teaching work. (It would be the first of many name changes over the years.)

They then explained that should any of us decide to join the community and sit with Bubba, we'd need to observe specific conditions, adding, "These conditions aren't rigid rules — Bubba calls them 'absolute recommendations.'"

The first condition was a "life-enhancing vegetarian diet consistent with spiritual practice." *So far, so good*, I thought, just before they added that the diet included "the elimination of all processed sweets such as ice cream, doughnuts, pastries, and chocolate." Given my sweet tooth, that was going to be a challenge. I made a mental note to buy a doughnut on the way home, since it might be my last one, at least for a while. (I wasn't making any lifetime commitments.)

Second, everyone in the community was to practice "a non-promiscuous relationship to sexuality and an economy of sexual release. In other words, as Bubba has said, 'Unless you're married, keep it in your pants.'"

Other conditions included morning calisthenics and an afternoon or evening yoga routine as well as holding a full-time job and tithing 10 percent of monthly income — "a customary form of support in many religious communities," our host added.

I'd also need to move into one of the many community households in San Francisco and contribute to the rent, food, and household duties. "Living in a household," they explained, "provides support for maintaining the conditions and discussing the Guru's teachings with other devotees."

They continued: "Every weekend, households carpool up to the Mountain of Attention Sanctuary in Clearlake Highlands to sit with the Guru as well as practice *guru seva*, or service to the Guru and community, suited to one's skills…" *Which means no more free weekends or weeknights, either*, I thought, since they had stated that evenings were devoted to study or service duties. Kicking back and relaxing were no longer options.

In closing this introduction, the couple explained that these requirements helped to "establish a stable foundation for spiritual practice. And most important, they represent a moment-to-moment surrender of self-will."

It's one thing to say, "Thy will be done," but it's another thing to live it, I thought. The Guru was asking for something I'd never considered before: submission to a higher will and wisdom, which both challenged and concerned me. I'd be sacrificing my privacy and, to some degree, my autonomy. Still, if this was a cult, it at least sounded like a wholesome one.

As I left the bookstore I saw a quotation by the Guru posted on the wall: "Before you can become spiritual, you have to become fully human."

Overwhelmed and a little numb, I let this new information sink in. The rare opportunity offered by the Guru and his community felt unique; so did the conditions. I'd be entering a full-time immersion unlike anything I'd encountered in the Arica School.

Real-World Challenges

After the bookstore talk, back in my empty apartment and self-imposed solitude, I considered all that I'd heard: The conditions themselves seemed reasonable. There was nothing weird to push against or criticize. But following this daily-life yoga meant surrendering a willful, independent nature closely tied to my identity.

While the Professor had asked me to observe and analyze my psyche, the Guru seemed to demand that I change my behavior from day one. His community was not cloistered in an ashram but intermingled with the world. Given my sense of being adrift, maybe this was my version of settling down. I needed to find a job anyway. Why not in San Francisco? Besides, I expected that the food would be more nutritious than what they served in the Navy.

A few days later, with the knowledge that my former wife and my daughter were settled into a stable homelife, I applied to join a community household. They invited me as a dinner guest, and I moved in a few days later. I then found work as a typist at a new office that wouldn't open for six weeks, so I was off the hook until then. *And*, I figured, *if this thing doesn't work out, I can always walk away.*

In the meantime, based on what I knew, and the promise of

spending time with a transcendental master, I might experience a radical approach to liberation in the presence of the Guru.

A Companion for Life

In August 1975 the Guru's admonition to get married or practice celibacy prompted one of the most important, crazy-wise decisions of my life: I called Joy and asked her if she would read the Guru's first three books and consider joining me in California. *And why wouldn't she leave her home and a possible career to join me?* I thought. *After all, I'm quite the catch: a twenty-nine-year-old former this-and-that, currently unemployed member of what might seem like some sort of cult. How could she refuse?*

She said she'd get back to me.

Joy's Memories

When I graduated in June and moved back to my parents' house in New Jersey, I had little sense of personal ambition or direction, having spent most of life helping someone. As a child, I worked in my parents' stationery store after school and on weekends. I played a large role in taking care of my younger sister. The summer of my sixteenth year, I ran the store along with one assistant because my mother had hurt her back and my father had a second job.

When my older brother, then at Harvard Medical School, was seriously injured by a drunk driver, I spent the summer of my junior year with my parents and sister in Cambridge, near Massachusetts General Hospital, helping them cope. So I wasn't accustomed to directing my life; I just went where I was most needed. How different Dan's life seemed to be, making his own choices and pursuing his own dreams.

When I left Oberlin, I didn't know if I'd ever see Dan again. This left a huge void in my life. I ended up enrolling in the Arica advanced training, then drove to Milwaukee to live and teach in an Arica house — a way to be spiritually closer to Dan. We didn't correspond for months, since he was still trying to salvage what was left of his marriage.

When I learned that Dan, Linda, and six-year-old Holly had left Oberlin and returned to Berkeley, California, I let him know that a few Arica friends and I had decided to drive west on vacation and that we'd soon visit the Bay Area. I ended up having dinner with Dan and Linda at their apartment. Everyone was cordial, yet there was something in the air. *Maybe I just imagined it. We've moved on*, I told myself. *All is well with their marriage, and I can move on too.*

I decided it was time to leave the Arica house and return to New Jersey. I needed to make some money and consider my options. My dad offered to get me a job at DuArt Media, a film lab in Manhattan, where he was the night manager. We commuted together every weekday afternoon. I could tell that my dad enjoyed having company on these drives to and from work. He planned to have me learn film editing, thinking he was setting me up for a career.

During the summer of 1975, Dan and I began a regular correspondence. In July he wrote that he and Linda had separated and that they were going through a divorce. Soon after that, Dan asked me to read some books by an author and teacher named Franklin Jones (or maybe his name was Bubba Free John by that time). I was intrigued but also intimidated by his teaching.

Arica had been challenging, but when the training was over, it was over; there were no daily rules or requirements about how I lived my life. This guru was different, with numerous conditions affecting everyday life. I wasn't prepared for that type of commitment. Meanwhile, Dan and I kept writing. Then, in August, he invited me to come to California to live with him. I thought it over for about a week. In the end, I knew I wanted to be with Dan.

When I told my parents that I planned to leave, the house became as quiet as a morgue. After giving DuArt the requisite two weeks' notice, I continued to commute in with my father, who barely spoke to me.

In early September, after I said goodbye to my mother and sister, my dad drove me to the airport on his way to work. After a quick goodbye, he pulled away. He never even got out of the car. I knew my parents were disappointed that I was leaving again. They had no idea about what to think of Dan or my relationship with him. I felt sadness and guilt about leaving my family and some doubts about my future.

The Beginning of Forever

As summer drew to a close, Joy called me and said she was at the airport. "In New Jersey?" I asked. "You're coming?"

"In San Francisco," she said. "I've arrived."

On the way back from the airport, Joy told me that she'd read the Guru's books and had serious reservations. I could empathize; I had reservations of my own.

After a brief trip to visit my parents in Los Angeles, then a visit with Holly, Joy and I settled into our respective jobs and the rhythms of our community household, which included two other women and one man on Masonic Street in the Haight-Ashbury district. We carpooled every Friday evening up to the sanctuary near Clearlake, about a two-hour drive north.

That's where we were married, on a Saturday night in October, in a simple but elegant ceremony witnessed by a few members of our household. Joy wore a garland of flowers in her hair, her large eyes shining. I wore my best sweater. This time, our marriage felt not only right but inevitable. I'd found the love of my life. And from the moment I said "I do," my commitment to Joy was even greater than my bond to the Guru, and always would be.

Though we had our own bedroom, we were otherwise in a fishbowl, conscious of being observed by our housemates as we observed them. We cultivated our couplehood while doing our best to avoid what the Guru termed "a cult of pairs," in which couples lived a secret life with a fire wall between them and the rest of their household.

Meanwhile, no matter which way I turned, I ran straight into the Guru's life conditions, which revealed my adolescent tendencies to live according to my inclinations, something I'd previously called freedom. Daily life had become a frustrating, productive, and sustainable spiritual boot camp.

Joy's Memories

After a few weeks together and once we'd joined a community household, life became more complicated. Dan had so many ideas and a great desire to influence people. He had a genuineness about him that I'd sensed when I first met him. Due to my profound faith in Dan, I was willing to join the community as an experiment. People did things like that in the 1970s.

When Dan and I married, it felt like a natural and inevitable thing to do.

Our first months in the community were intense, as we both aimed to follow all the conditions to the letter. Dan was especially rigorous. I soon noticed that the people around us were much more lax regarding the conditions, and that no higher-ups were paying attention anyway. This didn't change our behavior.

The Heat of Practice

I now understood the difference between the Arica trainings and sitting in the presence of a fully awakened transmitter of illumination for anyone open to receiving it. Joy and I arrived at the sanctuary every Friday night, found a sleeping space, and then checked our posted Saturday work assignments. Saturday evening was usually reserved for a movie that Bubba had selected, adding his hilarious commentaries and instructive lessons related to the film. But Sunday morning brought the main event: *darshan* with the Guru in the communion hall.

Once everyone had taken their places, waiting in anticipation, the Guru entered. We all bowed, touching our heads to the floor as he walked up to his large chair. Then, along with all the others in the room, I gazed at him for about an hour, doing my best to apply *feeling-attention*, as he'd recommended. At times his eyes filled with tears as his gaze moved about the room, momentarily alighting on each of us. As much as I'd tried to whip up a devotional fervor, to submit and surrender, I felt as if I were an actor playing the role of a loving devotee.

Whenever I tried anything new in my life, I'd dive into it wholeheartedly and enthusiastically, suspending judgment or disbelief, and see where it would lead and what I might learn. In truth, Joy and I were better students than devotees. Still, I couldn't deny a certain brightness and restless energy I felt in my immersion with the Guru.

A few of the devotees in the communion hall manifested spontaneous *kriyas* — rushes of energy with seizurelike shaking, grunts, and involuntary facial contortions — a phenomenon envied by some, since such displays seemed to indicate profound devotional surrender. Other devotees attributed dreams, insights, and emotional or even physical healing to the Guru, even though he discouraged such talk. It was all *lila*, or divine play, to him, and he made light of such phenomena, saying, "These peculiar people need to eat more grounding food."

The Seven Stages

A few weeks later, the Guru outlined what he called the seven stages of life, a hierarchical model of the evolution of consciousness, which, unsurprisingly, put his level of realization into its proper context. The first three stages each take seven years: first, physical embodiment, then emotional-sexual development, then higher mental functions culminating in a strong will, ideally by twenty-one years of age. Few humans emerge fully mature or prepared for the later stages.

The fourth, fifth, and sixth stages (which have no time frame) are dependent on the first three and represent "becoming fully human." The fourth stage manifests as a transition from gross to subtle levels of being, a natural urge to love and serve (but where God is still viewed as an "other"). The fifth, or mystical, stage of life is characterized by absorption in light, wherein spiritual or psychic experiences and ecstatic visions may appear.

Sixth-stage realizers such as Jesus, Buddha, Muhammad, and lesser-known figures like Ramana Maharshi abide in and as consciousness itself, free of any apparent conditions or limitations.

The Guru claimed that he alone had attained the seventh stage, which he described as "a new possibility where there exists no separation, only God."

His message was that no search is necessary; that there is nothing to be achieved but only realized — we need only awaken to what is "always, already the case." This transcendent message, expressed in the pages of his early works, had first drawn me to the Guru like a moth to the flame.

New Teachings

The Guru's ability to transmit a spiritual force drew many devotees. But his insightful teachings were the primary draws for me. For example, he once referred to three types of people: Solids (or serious folks, with a "stone in their navel"); Vitals (expansive, energetic types, "with a fire in their navel"), and Peculiars (more classical spiritual types, "with a hole in their navel"). Each of these types related differently to bodily life and spiritual teachings. (I was an easily recognizable Solid and Joy a Vital.) These clear, simple, yet profound observations generated the self-awareness I'd sought in my psychology studies.

On another occasion the Guru described three approaches to teachers, teachings, and authority figures that corresponded to stages of life: childhood, adolescence, and adulthood. Those in the childhood of spiritual development, he said, treated him like an idealized parent who can instruct, set limits, protect, and guide them. He added, "There's nothing wrong with this childlike stage, but you must eventually grow out of it." The adolescent stage entails a rejection of any authority with a corresponding need to make independent decisions. The adolescent mind views any authority with suspicion, and all spiritual teachers as charlatans and hucksters. Adults find wisdom wherever it may appear, not automatically accepting or rejecting what they read or hear, but weighing it against their own discernment.

Hearing this helped me appreciate the Guru more, since I'd encountered and bypassed other teachers who encouraged a childlike devotion. I recalled moments when I'd behaved like a naïve child and other moments when I'd acted like a rebellious adolescent. It seemed that I was now evolving toward a more mature approach to the Guru and to all spiritual teachings. In any event, everyone in the community was expected to transcend rather than merely analyze, resist, or indulge these habitual strategies of relating to the world.

Divine Ignorance

A few months later, on a typical weekend at the sanctuary (if there was such a thing), a simple question from the Guru set in motion a deep contemplation that led to another *kensho* — a breakthrough like the one I'd experienced at the Arica advanced training when I realized that everything was indeed my dream.

It began as the Guru sipped from a glass of water, then held up the glass and asked, "Can someone tell me what this is?" This simple question with a seemingly obvious answer turned into a six-week immersive contemplation of a new facet of his teaching work, which he called "The Way of Divine Ignorance," based on the observation that even as humanity amasses an expanding body of knowledge, no one — not teachers or doctors or intellectuals or even spiritual masters — knows what a single thing is.

Holding up his glass, and delivering a long Socratic dialogue to those gathered, the Guru continued to repeat the same question, asking if someone could tell him what it is. People tried different approaches — it's a glass...a drinking vessel...a silicate crystalline structure — until the Guru responded: "Yes, we could write encyclopedias, a torrent of words *about* the name, labels, description, construction, chemistry, aesthetics, and history of a glass, yet we remain completely ignorant about its essence — what it *is*. You are unburdened of knowing, free of meanings, you see..."

Over the course of several weeks, this ongoing contemplation burned in my belly like a koan until, all at once, I got a taste of it, a glimpse, just a glimmer; a realization broke through that beyond word labels, I didn't (and couldn't) know what anything actually *was*.

There's a monumental difference between an intellectual grasp or appreciation of this notion and the *realizing* of it, if only for a moment. And in that moment, it felt like liberation, and life became a mystery unfolding.

Guru's Teaching, Guru's Touch

As my primary form of service up at the sanctuary, and occasionally at the bookstore in San Francisco, I transcribed many of the Guru's talks to the community. These talks were given titles such as "Sex, Laughter, and God Realization" and "The Two-Sided Man or Woman."

After our first two intensive months in the community, while typing in a backroom office at the community bookstore one evening, I was surprised to see the Guru himself enter the small room where I sat typing. I remember thinking, *What are the protocols? Should I stand and face him, like meeting the Queen or, well, Moses? Should I continue with my work or remain seated and continue typing?* I ended up swiveling slightly around and nodding in a friendly, respectful way.

As the Guru passed me, he paused and gave me a brief shoulder rub, as if to acknowledge the work I was doing. Then, without a word, he continued on his way. I took a deep breath, checking to see if my body felt different, if anything magical or spiritual had occurred, some special blessing. It felt as if a loving friend had touched me as a natural human connection, nothing more.

I soon turned back to my typing, thinking: *If someone had told me earlier in the day that before the day was out the Guru was going to give me a back rub, I'd have laughed out loud.*

Joy's Memories

Our relationship to the community had ups and downs. Living with other people and going up to the sanctuary every weekend took a toll, not only on the two of us but on many devotees, which is how people in the community referred to themselves. Life with Da Free John, as he now called himself, was demanding and sometimes disturbing. He aimed to shake us out of ourselves. He was a constant intrusion and interruption in my life and personal desires. Dan and I spent many hours going over the pros and cons of staying or leaving.

Looking back, I had my first inkling that there was something wrong. This sense provoked a deeper understanding that I had an inner knower — a gut feeling that I could weigh things against — and maybe I would be wise to trust myself more than I trusted Da Free John. This experience would later help me develop my ability to discern the good and bad of any situation.

Coming and Going

Midweek, in another unpredictable change, all households received the same announcement: "All conditions are suspended. Live wherever and however you want." Was this more of the Guru's crazy-wisdom experimental theater, or was the community disbanding? The conditions and households had been such an integral way of life, and a constant reminder of the Guru, and I felt a mix of disappointment, uncertainty, and relief.

Prior to this announcement, Joy and I hadn't had any leisure time to be together as a young married couple, and I'd been unable to visit with Holly, who had since moved north with her mom and her new stepfather to Grass Valley, California.

Now, in another stroke of good timing, I learned of a teaching position at a small gymnastics studio on Clement Street in San Francisco. I met with Christine, the studio owner. She couldn't pay much, but if I agreed to teach four evening classes a week, she offered to include a small, rent-free apartment directly above the studio. So Joy and I departed from our Masonic Street household and moved into our own cozy apartment. As I began teaching teen and adult gymnastics classes, Joy landed a job as a payroll clerk at a downtown accounting firm.

We would never again be as immersed in community life or visit the sanctuary every weekend as we had in the beginning. But the Guru maintained a presence in my life and awareness (and in Joy's), especially through his new books, which were published at a prolific pace, expressing his unique insights on conscious exercise and diet, human sexuality, awakened politics, enlightenment of the whole body, and the transcendent meaning of death. Even if he had never taken on the mantle of a spiritual master, the Guru's literary output would have been a significant contribution.

Joy and I still visited the sanctuary on occasion, even though the Guru now spent much of his time either partying with his inner circle or in seclusion. He changed his name again and would do so several more times in the descending arc of his career.

I'd later ask myself why we remained associated with the community for nearly eight years. As was the case with my first marriage, I couldn't fully commit or let go. Maybe it was due to sheer persistence, or because a community of sincere spiritual aspirants seemed preferable to the crazy secular world of the late 1970s. Maybe it was also due to simple inertia; we stayed until a better alternative appeared. So, as the months, then years passed, each time we distanced ourselves physically or emotionally, we were drawn back in.

Meanwhile, teaching evening classes at the gymnastics studio left me the daytime hours to work more seriously on an as-yet-untitled manuscript filled with random perspectives from my years as an athlete and martial artist, along with larger themes inspired by the Professor and now the Guru. Rather than merely parroting elements of their teachings, I strove to create my own manner of expression in everyday language. It hadn't yet occurred to me to include elements from my own life, but gradually the material took shape.

Whatever the circumstances, I still loved to teach, but the content and scope of my interest had expanded. Recalling a quotation by the Indian sage Ramana Maharshi that the Guru had shared with us — "I give people what they want until they want what I want to give them" — I continued teaching acrobatic skills. But I found great satisfaction whenever a student expressed an interest in movement as a path to mastery.

Someone wrote me to say how much he'd enjoyed reading the Guru's first book but expressed concern about the "complications and obstructions," and his own lack of "feeling-attention."

My response, which uses community jargon, reveals my state of mind at that time, and demonstrates how I went all-in, immersing myself in whatever path or person I followed:

> Don't be concerned. Take care of business so you can free up feeling-attention necessary for equanimity. You'll never get it perfect. Just use whatever arises as *sadhana* (spiritual practice). Any fool can be happy when things are going smoothly. Practice unreasonable happiness by remembering what is prior to all these apparent complications, just stuff within the dream. Make your first priority *understanding*.
>
> No one else makes us mad or glad or sad or fearful or excited, no matter how much it seems to be so. You and I create meanings and interpretations about reality. If someone knocked on your door and handed you a tax-free cashier's check for one million dollars, you might jump up and down with happiness. But you could have experienced the same happiness before that knock on the door. That man only gave you a reason.
>
> Spiritual life is about finding the place where you are always, already happy and free, prior to whatever you do to obstruct it. That's why *understanding* is so important. Until you and I see all our habitual tendencies, and transcend them, spiritual life remains an idea of the intellect, a belief, a hopeful but rote practice.

In a sense I was writing to myself, for myself. Rereading that bit of correspondence, I smiled, thinking of several sayings that described my shaky role at the time: As an aikido proverb goes, "Learn one day, teach one day." In other words, even beginners benefit themselves and others by teaching what they've just learned. And a saying passed around by medical interns and residents about surgeries also applies: "Watch one, do one, teach one." In truth, I was testing out a new role — watching, doing, teaching.

Changes in Time

A year passed quickly on Clement Street, with my days spent writing and my evenings spent teaching acrobatics to children and adults. Occasionally, Joy and I visited the sanctuary, but otherwise had little contact with the community as I focused on more worldly matters. Then, at year's end, we bid a fond farewell to Christine and moved across the bay into a basement apartment in the Berkeley hills near the rose garden.

That spring of 1978 I'd applied for the position of women's gymnastics coach at Cal. (While no longer enamored with the competitive enterprise, I needed a job consistent with my talents and teaching experience.) On my way to the interview, I bought two reams of typing paper because my single manuscript had since split into two different books. The first book, drawn from my years as an athlete and coach, was nearly complete. I titled the second book, still in development, *Way of the Peaceful Warrior.*

Coaching the Cal women's team turned out to be tougher than I'd anticipated. With no dedicated space of our own, we had to set up all the equipment at the beginning of each workout, then break it down at the end. I did the best I could with the team, which ended that first year with an undistinguished season.

After running on the Strawberry Canyon trails, Joy and I ran the seven-mile Bay to Breakers run from the Ferry Building on the bay side, up "Heartbreak Hill," then due west through San Francisco to the surf at Ocean Beach — a loony run alongside people dressed as centipedes or in drag, with some wearing nothing at all. And later that summer, we aimed to complete the first San Francisco Marathon, nearly missing the commemorative T-shirt truck before it pulled away. Elated and exhausted, we managed to lift our arms for a high five, although few spectators remained to see our triumph. After that, Joy continued running the trails. I still ran, but most of my energy went into rewriting and refining the two manuscripts.

A Rewarding Routine

Later that summer, when our landlord sold the house, we moved once again, down to the flatlands of Berkeley to a converted garage studio, a quiet, cozy nest furnished with a sofa Joy had made with foam and cloth and a loft bed I'd constructed. During that yearlong stay, and my second year of coaching, we settled into a productive routine: Joy ran in the mornings before work. I dove into immersive writing from eight a.m. to noon, before heading to the women's gym.

After polishing my *Whole Body Fitness* manuscript, I mailed it to one New York publisher after the next. Each time it was returned unopened, without explanation, until one editorial assistant took the time to scrawl across the package, "We only accept work sent by a literary agency." So I looked in the phone directory and found the Larsen-Pomada agency in San Francisco. After reading the manuscript, Michael and Elizabeth sent me a one-page agency agreement.

A few weeks later, when I was at my desk in the athletic department office, my agent called and informed me that Crown Publishing in New York had offered five thousand dollars (worth about twenty thousand dollars today) as an advance against future royalties. I was a writing professional! I still recall Mike Larsen's timeless words of advice to a new author: "Don't quit your day job yet."

Despite good moments, my second year as women's coach was another uphill climb. Near the end of our season, after the team had put away the equipment, I sat alone atop a stack of mats, contemplating the question: *What would Buddha or Jesus or Socrates do in this situation?* An inner voice answered, *Junior, they wouldn't be in this situation.* I had to face the fact that my heart was no longer in coaching. So, despite my literary agent's sage advice, I did quit my day job, informing the athletic director that I wouldn't be returning for a third year. (The coach who followed me, a female Olympian, lasted only one year.) I then contacted the Oberlin College dean of housing and applied for a dorm director's position, signaling our desire to rejoin the college community where we'd met and our readiness to leave our current community behind.

As *Whole Body Fitness* moved through the publishing process that transformed a manuscript into a finished book, I began yet another rewrite of *Way of the Peaceful Warrior.*

The Fruits of My Labor

In early July 1979, as we prepared for our road trip back to Oberlin, *Whole Body Fitness* was published, garnering positive reviews. (In the coming years, the book would be published under three different titles, changing names nearly as many times as the Guru until its current title: *Body Mind Mastery.*)

Meanwhile, I completed what I thought would be the final draft of *Way of the Peaceful Warrior,* which at that point included just a page or two about meeting a cosmic old gas station mechanic — the rest read like a nonfiction self-help guidebook. I sent the manuscript to my agent. He called a few weeks later to tell me he'd received another offer of five thousand dollars, this time from Jeremy P. Tarcher in Los Angeles. Thrilled, I accepted, even as Joy and I packed our few belongings into a small rental truck and left for Oberlin in optimistic spirits. Now flush with cash from the second book advance, we'd have free room and board and a small stipend.

The edited manuscript arrived soon after we did. I tore open the package to find marked-up pages with comments and queries. My editor Janice Gallagher was enthusiastic about the book but wanted to know more about Socrates and my interactions with him. Inspired by her edits, I careened into a frenzied, immersive rewrite. While Joy took care of all dorm duties, I cloistered myself in the back room up to eighteen hours a day, in an elevated adrenal state, fleshing out a story based on my life, adding imagined late-night meetings with the old peaceful warrior. All my experiences and summary insights over the past ten years went into those pages. I included the Professor's bone massage, and adapted the Guru's notion of unreasonable happiness and his reference to "paradox, humor, and change," as well as his comment that "the secret of change is to focus your energy not on fighting the old but on building the new."

Then I mailed the final draft back to my editor.

Dark Horizon

When the Guru moved to a new sanctuary in Hawaii, Joy and I were also moved to a more critical assessment of this crazy-wisdom teacher, and of the behaviors that may have driven him into exile.

I later studied a variety of spiritual communities in which charismatic spiritual authorities devolved over time, corrupted by the adulation of their devotees. Like the boiling frog effect, incremental changes in someone's personality can remain unnoticed, ignored, or denied until the reality is inescapable. The lives of many contemporary spiritual teachers are object lessons, and the Guru was unfortunately an exemplar of this phenomenon — a valuable lesson that he never intended.

Despite his extraordinary spiritual gifts, the Guru had outsized vices foreshadowed early on. This paradoxical spiritual master and brilliant author was also a likely alcoholic, drug user, and serial philanderer, having slept with numerous women in the community along with the nine polygamous partners he called his "wives," one of whom was a *Playboy* Playmate of the Month, a good-natured young woman who'd arrived at the sanctuary with her boyfriend but who was soon living in the Guru's home.

For years, the Guru's activities remained as background within his community. We all knew that he was not a white-robed celibate preaching morality, and we accepted him as an unconventional teacher whose behavior was presumed to be instructive, for the sake of his devotees. I'd also heard accounts from credible witnesses to the Guru's Saturday night parties, where a handful of the Guru's inner circle and invited guests joined his wild affairs, where all conditions were abandoned in his company. Credible sources spoke of tantric orgies in which the Guru instructed devotees to have sex with one another and with himself while other revelers watched, and as alcohol, tobacco, and other drugs circulated freely.

Whether this wild theater of uninhibited play was exploration or exploitation, I can't say for certain. I only remember how everyone at the sanctuary was asked to be especially quiet when passing the Guru's residence on Sunday mornings so as not to disturb his sleep.

When the Guru visited the old sanctuary in Northern California, I noted how his appearance had changed — his body rounder and his complexion wan as if from hard living. He started going on fasts and undergoing various purifications and treatments. In one talk he spoke of the great sacrifice he made by reflecting his devotees' subhuman behavior.

Our time with the Guru had unfolded in a particular place and time, within a community of good-hearted devotees, and in the changing atmosphere of the 1970s and early 1980s as we stumbled together, through flickering shadows, toward the light.

Changing Fortunes

I wrote *Way of the Peaceful Warrior* to bridge the conventional and transcendent dimensions of life. Since the book blended autobiography with fictional elements, my editor suggested the subtitle *A Basically True Story* — a clever idea, but the book-chain buyers had no idea whether to shelve the book in fiction or nonfiction, or in Religion, Psychology, Philosophy, Metaphysics, Occult, or any established spiritual tradition. Only a few thousand copies were sold by independent bookstores. Despite a number of enthusiastic letters my editor received, the publisher declined to print a paperback edition, so publishing rights returned to me.

About the same time, I learned that *Whole Body Fitness* had sold about four thousand copies before also going out of print. Having tasted success as a college student-athlete, coach, and college professor, I was now the author of two out-of-print books. When I asked my agent if he could reach out to other publishers, he offered the standard advice: "Write another book, Dan. If it sells well, maybe someone will pick up the others."

I toyed with a few half-baked writing ideas that didn't pan out; my heart wasn't in them. So I practiced aikido a few evenings a week and helped Joy with dorm duties.

Our two years at Oberlin, along with my previous time on the faculty, hold a special place in my memory: I met Joy, honed my teaching skills, completed *Way of the Peaceful Warrior*, and saw the birth of our daughter Sierra there, fourteen years after I'd wandered into the old service station in Berkeley.

Then the most intriguing thing happened: From the few hardbound copies still in circulation, word of mouth began to build for *Way of the Peaceful Warrior*. Yet I wouldn't write another book for nearly ten years, until circumstances compelled me to do so.

Life Goes On

In the spring of 1981, as our two-year dorm director position drew to a close, Joy and little Sierra and I returned to the San Francisco Bay Area, this time to Marin County. We had no further desire to see the Guru, who was by then living mostly in Hawaii, but we still had some community friends in San Rafael, where I found work as a word-processing operator in a management training firm. When that job ended a year later, due to corporate downsizing, I found a nine-to-five data entry position at a real estate firm and a second job on Saturday evenings and six a.m. most weekdays doing overload typing at a San Rafael law firm.

Then, as one of my ever-changing day jobs, I found an administrative position at an innovative bodywork school. It was my job to recruit local folks interested in serving as models on whom students could practice under the founder's supervision. Late one Friday afternoon, I pushed myself to meet a self-imposed deadline. Feeling stressed out, I rushed to complete phone calls and fill out forms before Joy and Sierra arrived to pick me up for the weekend. My breathing shallow, I felt a pressure rising, building toward a headache.

Just then, I glanced out the window to see a single cloud floating gently, patiently, on the breeze. I felt myself take a long, deep breath and relax my entire body. Feeling like that cloud, I completed my work at an even, unhurried pace, before the end of the workday. *Our teachers are everywhere*, I thought. That was the first insight. The second insight came only when I realized that even after all the deep relaxation and breathwork I'd practiced in Arica, it could take months or years to fully integrate and apply what I'd learned, and to embody those lessons in daily life.

Our Family Is Completed

Sierra, now two years old, liked to pull books out of our bookcase and open them. Since the Guru's books were within her reach, she opened the same book several times to look at a particular photo of him as he sat gazing into the transcendent.

When I asked Sierra what he was looking at, she said, "Looking at bird."

Joy and I both smiled at this cute but puzzling response. That autumn of 1982, Joy was well into her pregnancy with our second child. To prepare Sierra, we'd given her a small stuffed panda bear with a baby panda tucked inside the mother, explaining that mommy also had a baby in her tummy, and when it was born, Sierra would have a new sister or brother. She seemed to grasp this, but it was hard to know for certain.

One evening at dinner, I asked Sierra who she was before she was a little girl. "I was a baby," she answered.

"That's right. And where were you before you were a baby?"

"In Mama's tummy," she said.

Then, on impulse, I asked, "Where were you *before* you were in Mama's tummy?"

Without any hesitation, she said, "Looking at bird." Somehow, Sierra had associated the Guru's gaze with where she was before she was conceived.

Later, Joy recalled that when she was in labor with Sierra,

doing Lamaze breathing and preparing to push, she peered intently at an image on a nearby box of tissues — a photo of a bird in flight.

Then, on a stormy evening in February 1983, Joy, assisted by a midwife in our bedroom at home, gave birth to our second daughter, whom we named China. Just after the delivery I brought a sleepy-eyed Sierra into the room to meet her newborn sister. She looked at China with eyes of wonder, perhaps thinking it was a dream.

A few weeks later, I founded Rent-a-Coach, a new venture in line with my experience as an athlete and coach. As a personal fitness trainer, I drove to clients' homes and led them through custom workouts. During this period, Holly, now in her teens and busy with her own life up in Grass Valley, was able to visit me, Joy, and her two little stepsisters — a welcome gathering of my three daughters.

Distancing and Departure

As the years passed, Joy and I maintained a connection to the Guru's community as Friends of the Work, which enabled our daughters to attend the community preschool and kindergarten. Their teachers seemed devoted to nurturing the children. Listening to and reading stories about male and female saints in different traditions, eight-year-old Sierra found positive role models in Anandamayi Ma and Sarada Devi, two Hindu saints. And an inspired little China, still in preschool, woke up one morning singing, "Daolaloma, he awakens me up!" Our girls both benefited from life-affirming role models they wouldn't have encountered in regular schools, so we could understand why some Catholic or other Christian or Jewish parents preferred parochial schools.

On the darker side, spiritual instruction for children can easily become indoctrination rather than education.

Mostly to see some familiar friends, Joy and I attended a few Sunday gatherings in Marin, which felt like church meetings with a Hindu twist. At one such gathering, we were pleased to see on display a new framed photograph of an empty chair, representing the true guru as a nameless divine spirit with whom anyone could commune. Each household was instructed to place this photo of the empty chair in their personal meditation area as a reminder that the divine is formless and omnipresent, consistent with the Guru's original teachings.

But the very next week, in an abrupt turnaround, we were all told to replace the image of the empty chair with a photo of the Guru himself, once again an object of worship, sitting in that same chair — a profoundly disappointing reversal. No longer a living presence or universal teacher, the Guru now seemed a tired and distorted shadow of the light I'd first encountered nearly a decade before. It would be the final community gathering that either of us would attend.

Soon after, we transferred our daughters to a local Montessori school, where they thrived.

A Literary Rebirth

In the summer of 1982, while attending a weekend Neuro-Linguistic Programming (NLP) workshop, I gave a spare hardback copy of *Way of the Peaceful Warrior* to an older woman who'd expressed an interest in "that sort of book." After she read it, she later told me, she passed it on to her seventy-year-old friend Hal Kramer, a retired publisher. After reading it, Mr. Kramer decided to create a new publishing company on a shoestring budget, beginning with my book.

He invited me to lunch and asked me for permission to re-publish the book as a paperback. Now more sophisticated, having previously earned an advance of five thousand dollars for each of my books, I asked, "How much of an advance are you prepared to pay me?"

"Um, how about a hundred dollars?" he said.

"Hmm...and how much do you plan to spend on marketing and promotion?"

"I'll write letters to the book chains and independent stores letting them know about the new paperback edition of your book."

"And how many people work at your publishing house?"

"Just me, at the moment," he answered.

I considered Hal's underwhelming offer for about five seconds before reaching out to shake his hand. "You've got a deal." It was, after all, the best (and only) offer I'd had in almost four years. Hal Kramer sent a simple contract to my agent, who strongly advised me to decline.

I signed anyway, in an act of faith that Hal and I would celebrate for many years to follow. As founder of the Celestial Arts publishing company in the 1960s, Hal had his finger on the pulse of the human potential movement. He understood my book and its readership. When I showed him the pile of letters I'd received, nearly all echoing the same phrase, Hal decided to use the provocative subtitle *A book that changes lives.*

It took Hal Kramer more than a year to convince the major book chains to take one copy to place in each store. He hand-sold the book, giving a copy to everyone he met. The book was met with a modest but enthusiastic group of readers who wanted more. As the months passed, word of mouth continued to build. Somehow, the words I wrote, reflecting my years of searching and study, had touched the hearts and minds of readers. This time around, the book's moment had arrived.

Joy's Memories

When we started receiving more letters about *Way of the Peaceful Warrior*, many people asked similar questions. It occurred to me that Dan could make an audiocassette with basic elements about his teaching. He recorded a ninety-minute program called *The Peaceful Warrior in Daily Life*. We wrote a one-page brochure about the cassette program and about a new workshop that Dan had designed.

After that, orders arrived almost daily. That recorded program not only answered most questions but also helped to pay for our groceries.

We stayed in Da Free John's community longer than we might otherwise have done so our daughters could attend the community's Big Wisdom School, which we thought at the time was a unique educational experience. As more news came out about Da Free John, we no longer wanted our daughters or us to be associated with the community, clearing the way for our departure.

Public Revelations

In 1985, when a former devotee and wife of a community officer sued the Guru for sexual abuse, an article broke in the *San Francisco Chronicle* titled "The Sex Guru." Even then some community members justified or dismissed this reality, either because they believed the allegations were overblown or thought that the Guru's behavior transcended conventional morality. But it was the beginning of the end. A significant number of disciples departed from the Guru's company when their family and friends grew concerned about their well-being and the sex guru label found traction among the general public.

The Guru had since moved from Hawaii to his island retreat in Fiji, where he remained in seclusion for several decades, visited only by selected devotees. But Joy and I had physically and emotionally left the Guru long before he left us.

In a dualistic world, we tend to see people, including spiritual teachers, as good or bad, kind or callous, wise or ignorant. But reality is paradoxical, not mutually exclusive. In many ways the Guru did behave like a crazy man even as he continued writing books that were quickly devoured by seekers and lauded by scholars.

And, yes, amid his increasingly bizarre behavior and divine hubris, the Guru used crazy wisdom as a transcendental get-out-of-jail-free card, having somehow missed the fact that in the conventional world, certain rules still apply. As Albert Schweitzer once wrote, "Example is not the main thing in influencing others, it is the only thing." Rather than serving as such an example, in the manner of Mahatma Gandhi, who famously said, "My life is my message," the Guru appeared to operate on a "Do as I say, not as I do" principle. This seemed not only hypocritical, but foolish, even for those willing to believe that the Guru's inner circle orgies were a tantric teaching or sexual-emotional catharsis.

If wisdom bestows the capacity to foresee the consequences of one's actions, the Guru was, at the very least, unwise, or, at worst, an exploitative, self-indulgent sexual abuser.

When some community members caught a cold or flu, they attributed it to the Guru's grace, and when they recovered, it was again the Guru's grace. When members of any sect, including mainstream religious groups, believe that everything a priest, rabbi, teacher, therapist, or guru says or does is done for their benefit or awakening, they're vulnerable to exploitation.

The Guru, once a young, bright-eyed spiritual teacher, was now nearly fifty years old, his once-abundant hair nearly gone, his expression weary, his round face and body reflecting a hedonistic, even dissolute lifestyle. Rajneesh, aka Osho or Bhagwan Rajneesh, as well as Yogi Bhajan, Swami Muktananda, and numerous other yogic and Buddhist masters had also fallen from grace despite their charisma and gifts. One devotee described Muktananda (in a striking similarity to Da Free John) as "an enlightened spiritual teacher and a practitioner...who also engaged in actions that were not ethical, legal, or liberatory with many disciples." So Adi Da, as the Guru came to be known, was not alone in riding an arc from brilliant teacher to craven exploiter.

As a friend and former community member said of the Guru, "He was a great spiritual master who would have benefited from an AA Twelve-Step Program." Some crazy-wisdom teachers like Adi Da devolve over time to express less wisdom and more crazy.

One example of the Guru's lapse was a growing tendency to capitalize more and more words in his writing, presumably to convey the Transcendent (rather than transcendent) ideas that infused his work. One extreme example of his grandiosity is this brief sample from *Aham Da Asmi*, a book he wrote later in his career: "Those who Do Not heart-Recognize Me and heart-Respond to Me-and who (Therefore) Are Without Faith In Me Do Not (and Cannot) Realize Me. Therefore, they (By Means Of their own self-Contraction From Me) Remain ego-Bound...."

After all the public revelations, some of our friends assumed that Joy and I had joined a cult. From one perspective, that's fair. But earlier in his work, the Guru had addressed this topic in a witty and lucid fashion, reminding us that if we define a cult as a group of people with a shared devotion to a teacher or other authority, or a band or athlete or political theory, then hundreds (if not thousands) of cults or sects large and small exist in the modern world, including mainstream sects of Christianity, Buddhism, Islam, and Judaism.

"The question," the Guru noted, "is not whether a group is a cult, but whether that cult is destructive and coercive, or voluntary and life-affirming."

He then observed, "You know this community isn't some nefarious cult because it's difficult to enter and easy to leave." That was true except for a thin thread that binds devotees to their chosen master — a psychological thread made of steel.

Breaking the Steel Thread

A grand mission avowed by many spiritual groups is saving human culture by illuminating the consciousness of a sufficient number of people. The Professor's school and the Guru's community express this mission in similar terms — that only by realizing our essential human unity can we reduce or eliminate the divisiveness, war, and political squabbles that afflict us to create a peaceful and productive society. This high-minded goal awaits us at the summit of human maturity. But between our current state of consciousness and the mountaintop, we pass through a dark forest of denial, fear, and other challenges along the way. Ideals are what we strive for; reality reflects who and how we are now.

I'd seen and studied how some cults welcome needy neophytes with open arms and so-called love bombs, such as smiles, hugs, attention, and affection. Certain groups, such as MSIA (Movement for Spiritual Inner Awareness) and Scientology also offer inspiring or fascinating entry-level courses to draw curious seekers deeper into the fold. But the nature of these same organizations can turn darker over time, and it can be extraordinarily difficult to leave. Disincentives for leaving can include interventions by other members, implied or actual threats, manipulation, ostracism, and sometimes physical constraint.

To the best of my knowledge, nothing like that occurred in the Guru's community.

Practically speaking, it *was* quite easy to leave. A devotee could simply move out of the household and return to the simpler demands of daily life. But the Guru hadn't acknowledged the psychological turmoil that departing members encounter — the steel thread that can bind even disenchanted members, a thread formed by their relationship with the Guru (as well as with long-time friends and housemates in the community).

The connection to a guru or other inspiring teacher is not a minor one. Many seekers had changed their lives and circumstances, made major sacrifices, even moved halfway around the world and left behind family and friends to be with their guru (as Jesus had encouraged his disciples to do). They did so because they believed with all their hearts that their guru was the best, or only, true path to awakening. (Few followers believe they've found the second-best master around.) Those who walk away re-enact Adam and Eve's departure from the Garden of Eden, turning their backs on God, missing the last train to salvation.

Da Free John himself once proposed four reasons why some people leave: Either they find flaws with the Guru, with the teaching, or with the community, or they may believe that the fault is their own — that they're not up to this way of life. But after nearly eight years in the community, I never heard the Guru give a fifth reason that someone might leave: It might simply be the wisest choice for them.

Self-respect was a scarce commodity in the Guru's community, and it's lacking in many religions that view members as sinners or lost sheep who need saving or liberation through intermediary authorities, holy books, systems, philosophies, or clerics who, by virtue of their presumed superior wisdom, supposedly know what's best for us better than we know for ourselves.

This pattern repeats itself again and again, even as the errant behaviors of some spiritual leaders remain hidden in the shadows.

Pointers along the Way

Author Elizabeth Lesser advised her readers to note the disparity between spiritual teachings and the behavior of the teachers.

Author, psychotherapist, and teacher Stephan Bodian encouraged seekers to trust their intuition and common sense, to question and doubt, to maintain firm boundaries, to be patient, to examine family issues (since many seekers come from alcoholic or dysfunctional families), to avoid sex with a spiritual teacher, and to deemphasize the significance of *siddhis* (or apparent spiritual powers). He has also cited qualities of good teachers, including humility; encouraging autonomy and inquiry; directness, honesty, authenticity, and clarity; practicing what they preach; and showing compassion and kindness.

These summary reminders helped me to avoid any involvement with other charismatic but shady or deluded teachers or groups, such as Scientology, the Rajneesh (Osho) community, Heaven's Gate, Children of God, Branch Davidians, Jim Jones and the Peoples Temple, John-Roger's MSIA, and other, more recent groups. Many good-hearted seekers were drawn to such organizations, and to gurus such as Swami Muktananda, Yogi Bhajan, and other spiritual leaders who may have begun with the best of intentions but who each, in their own way, fell from grace.

Finding a Way Forward

After two decades of preparation — learning to integrate the physical and spiritual realms — the time had come for me to express a teaching of my own: the peaceful warrior's way.

I had by then shifted my attention to family, living an ordinary life founded on principles and perspectives gleaned over the years. Learning had been the easy part; applying these principles in daily life was more challenging. But after the Arica work and years in (and out of) the Guru's community, Joy and I had a good start. It was an enduring journey that we'd made together.

We lived modestly as our income allowed, buying furniture and clothing at Goodwill. Our tiny black-and-white TV and VHS player sat on a wooden apple crate, and more than once we added up our loose change to rent the occasional video after the girls were asleep. But we were encouraged by *Way of the Peaceful Warrior*'s growing readership, plus cassette tape sales that supplemented income from my personal coaching service.

I had no immediate plans to write more books, since I felt I'd expressed what I had to share. But as a creative project, I began work on a screenplay adaptation of *Way of the Peaceful Warrior*, learning more with each new draft. I now found meaning in the simple things. No longer looking backward or forward, I gazed upward, filled with the faith that in times of need, a solution might appear by chance or by grace, but only after I'd set the stage and laid the foundations.

In the Guru's company I'd almost lost the divine spark that existed within me and in everyone else. No longer reliant on following a divine authority, I'd need to relearn how to trust my own inner wisdom. This felt-need arose as a yearning, a prayer, a question. And as with most of my sincere inner questions, the answer came in the form of another unexpected mentor waiting in the wings.

A Dialogue with Socrates

So it took you years to learn that lesson about following a God-man.

"You've got to stop sneaking up on me like that!"

Never left. I was standing by, waiting patiently.

"Since our last conversation?"

And during all those passing years.

"Then why didn't you *say* something? Give me advice? You're pretty good at that."

That's not how it works. I'm not here for you to trust me. I'm here to help you trust yourself.

"If I can't trust my muse, who can I trust?"

So what did you learn from your experiences with the Guru, Dan? Aside from reading his books and studying the lessons he taught.

"He was a living paradox — a source of higher wisdom whose debauchery and grandiosity served as a bad example."

Or maybe a great example of what can happen...

"You know, Soc, it's easy to paint a caricature of the Guru as just another charlatan. But he was also radiant in his peak years, and he attracted some high-minded people looking for a connection to the transcendent."

As you've said, Dan, all teachers are human, and all humans have flaws. Holy men and women are no exception.

"It was so sad and disappointing, though, to witness the arc of a man's life from a spiritual master to a ruined hermit-renunciate. But let me try and collect my thoughts —"

Good luck with that.

Ignoring his comment, I continued: "I think I understand the limits of the Professor's inner-directed spiritual exercises as well as the practice of surrendering my power and judgment to a guru or other authority figure. Any path depends on the student's openness and succeeds or fails depending on the traveler's readiness. That readiness, a certain openness, seems to matter more than the particular path."

So now you're doing some teaching of your own —

"As you know, I've been teaching in one form or another since I was a kid, with my friends on the trampoline and then in gymnastics. But I've begun to address larger topics."

Out of the cocoon, growing wings —

"I wouldn't put it like that — it's just that my interests expanded. But what am I telling you this for? You're already aware —"

Yes, but it's useful to reflect…

"The thing is, I'm not just teaching what I've read or heard from the Guru, or from the Professor before him. I've kept the most practical insights and set aside the rest. It's similar to the ten thousand quotations I've read over the years, selecting only those that speak to the human condition —"

That's all any teacher can do — offer perspectives, observations, reminders. Keep it practical. Down-to-earth.

"Which begs the question: What about the transcendental aspects of life? That's what I went searching for all that time with the Professor and then the Guru."

There's a place for the transcendent. Always will be. In the meantime, you have to take care of business here and now.

"Like that Ram Dass quote about cosmic bliss but remembering our postal code —"

The world reminds us every day, Soc mused.

I sighed. "It can be a difficult world at times…"

Sure. But if you don't lift any weights, you don't get any stronger.

"Spiritual weight lifting."

Every day. So, Dan, after the Professor, then all those years with the Guru, did you finally come up with a plan?

"I never had a plan — still don't. It's like that saying 'Live by faith, not design.' Who am I to know what should happen, or what will serve my highest good? I only know that for whatever reason, I'm driven to share what I've learned, what I've seen..."

The measure of teachers are their students —

"I believe that. Now I'll just have to wait and see what unfolds."

Which seems good enough for now. Always now...

Then silence.

Chapter 11

The Warrior-Priest

*The most beautiful adventures
are not those we go to seek.*

ROBERT LOUIS STEVENSON

On a Sunday evening, our phone started ringing. When I answered, a woman named Leni introduced herself and invited me to a free talk later that week, given by someone named Michael Bookbinder, whom she described as a teacher of martial arts, healing, and practical metaphysics. She added, "He's read your book [*Way of the Peaceful Warrior*] and would like to meet you."

As a courtesy, I thanked her and told her I'd check my calendar. Despite her intriguing description of this man, I had no interest in meeting another teacher, and I put her invitation out of my mind.

A few nights later, Joy said, "Wasn't that martial arts teacher speaking tonight at the women's club? Why not drop by?"

I'd forgotten about it, but since our girls were asleep and Joy had bookkeeping to do, I grabbed my jacket and drove the short distance to the local women's club. At the door, a smiling woman handed me two flyers — one about an evening seminar called The Three Selves and another advertising a two-weekend Warrior-Priest Training. I found a seat among about twenty people scattered around the room on folding chairs.

A murmur rose from the back of the room as Michael Bookbinder entered. A lean, athletic-looking guy about my age, with dark hair and a close-cut black beard, he wore a red headband across his brow, black martial arts pants, a black T-shirt with a red-and-black logo, and a nylon auto-racing jacket to complete the effect of a badass spiritual teacher. He struck me as someone I could relate to, the kind of guy who could be a good friend or dangerous adversary. When he gazed around the room and his eyes paused briefly on me, I felt a weird sense of recognition, as if I were seeing a long-lost brother.

He described an organization he called Search & Rescue International, whose primary mission, he said, was rescuing lost souls, including outliers who'd forgotten their own purpose here. The thought arose: *I wonder if I might be one of those?*

He then outlined several services and seminars he offered, including ways to recognize the outlier souls among us — ways he would share at his upcoming Warrior-Priest program. He also described an array of gut-level confidence courses such as stunt-car driving and knife fighting to teach centering and grace under pressure. Since his work blended martial arts with metaphysics, the term *warrior-priest* seemed to suit him well.

In contrast to the grand missions of the Professor and Guru, both aiming to enlighten humanity, the Warrior-Priest's work took place in the trenches of daily life. And where the Professor's maps, models, and theories were cerebral, the Warrior-Priest appealed on a visceral level. He didn't even use the word *enlightenment*, which at this point was fine with me. And I liked his advice to "Check anything you read or hear from me or anyone else against your own inner knower."

The more he spoke, the more I liked what I heard: I wasn't being asked to sign up for a lengthy and expensive multistage program or surrender to a higher source. He offered short, affordable talks on various topics plus a two-weekend Warrior-Priest Training to better prepare attendees to face real-world challenges in everyday life. Equally impressive, he offered a no-questions-asked, money-back guarantee.

While someone was asking a question, a man sitting just behind me who'd recognized me whispered, "Dan, I heard that Socrates is based on Michael Bookbinder. Is that true?"

I whispered back, "My book was first published five years ago. This is the first time I've seen this Bookbinder fellow."

When the Warrior-Priest's talk ended, his assistant Leni asked me to stick around so Michael and I could talk.

The Warrior-Priest and I spoke briefly, then exchanged contact information. A few days later, I invited him to our house for dinner, where he met Joy and read a bedtime story to Sierra and China. We were all charmed by his presence and style. He clearly enjoyed children, telling us how he missed his son from a brief marriage twenty years earlier. Thinking of Holly, I could empathize. Over time, I'd discover that Michael seemed to generate a larger-than-life excitement and sense of drama.

A few days later, I met several members of the support team who had worked with the Warrior-Priest in Los Angeles and in Boulder, Colorado — a handsome and chiseled fitness trainer and martial artist named John; an astute, dark-eyed former model named Karen; and a Latina woman warrior everyone called A. C. — each as impressive for their presence and clarity as anyone I'd met in the Professor's or Guru's communities.

Joy's Memories

Even though he expressed metaphysical ideas, I found Michael Bookbinder approachable and practical, as well as confident and charismatic. Since I'd never met Oscar, and only knew Da Free John as a figure on a platform, Michael was a refreshing change. You could talk to him, and he responded to you in a clear and direct manner.

As Dan sometimes says, Michael was like a guardian angel or big brother, there when you needed him but not in your way. No matter what he spoke about, he always seemed supportive and often inspiring. His students appeared to be nourished by his talks, more sure of themselves. Just what we needed after our time in Da Free John's community.

Dan and I both sensed that Michael was just passing through our lives.

The Three Selves

Over the next month, Joy and I attended several of Michael's talks, followed by his Warrior-Priest Training held in a private home, attended by about twenty people. He presented the content via what he called "raps" — short talks on various topics, including fresh views on meditation and other spiritual exercises (SEs, as he called them) and on diet and exercise.

He then outlined a simple, powerful map of his work and life, derived from the Hawaiian *kahuna* teachings. He called this map the three selves — three separate and distinct aspects of consciousness. According to the *Huna* cosmology, the soul enters each of us the moment the child is viable and takes its first breath. In addition to the soul, each of us has three selves — distinct aspects of consciousness: the Higher Self, the Conscious Self, and the Basic Self.

Michael described the Higher Self (which he claimed to see) as a "guardian angel, a radiant being of swirling color and light that we feel as inspiration and upliftment."

The Conscious Self, he explained, is our ego or identity, whose primary function is adapting to this present lifetime. While "the ego has a bad reputation in spiritual circles," he pointed out how in ancient times when someone misbehaved, they'd say, "The Devil made me do it," while today people blame the ego, a necessary part of our being. "Problems arise," he added, "when we identify *only* with the Conscious Self."

The Basic Self, also referred to as our subconscious mind, is associated with the belly or vital area. Michael likened it to "a powerful inner child, four-to-seven years old." Responsible for the physical body's maintenance, the Basic Self functions through the autonomic nervous system. "Like most children," he said, "the Basic Self is highly suggestible, imaginative, and fun loving. It enjoys humor and pleasure. This understanding alone can help to enhance energy, motivation, and confidence; it can also accelerate healing through what most people call *the placebo effect.*"

He added, "Basic Selves are here to evolve into Conscious Selves, and Conscious Selves are here to evolve into Higher Selves." This model of the three selves was only a model — like string theory, or Freud's ego, id, and superego, or Jung's *anima* and *animus*. But the Warrior-Priest's model had immediate and practical applications in daily life that I found more useful than the Professor's maps of the psyche.

Part of the Warrior-Priest's work involved strengthening the Basic Self and also opening channels of communication between the Basic Self, Conscious Self, and Higher Self. He explained, "If the Conscious Self dominates or ignores the Basic Self's needs, that inner child can go into rebellion, resulting in self-sabotage, illness, accidents, or, in extreme cases, death." His point being that everyone needs to occasionally indulge in a few cheap thrills now and then, and that vacations help maintain rapport between the Basic and Conscious Selves. *Maybe that's one reason the Guru periodically encouraged wild weekend parties*, I thought.

The Warrior-Priest didn't just theorize about how the Basic Self worked; he also applied this understanding in the form of dramatic stories that appealed to that visceral inner child. In one such example, he began: "Some years ago, I was backing into a parking space when the horn sounded from a car parked behind me. Thinking it was a mistake, I continued. When the horn sounded again, I got out of my car and approached the driver to ask if there was a problem. The window rolled down and a 12-gauge shotgun emerged, pointing directly at my face. The gunman said, 'Get out of here. Now.' I got in my car, then drove around the block just in time to see a masked man run out of the bank and jump into that car, which sped away. After that incident," Michael concluded, "I asked myself, What if the getaway driver had pulled the trigger — what unfinished business had I left undone? Who did I need to thank or tell that I loved them?"

All the Warrior-Priest's stories were like that — dramatic and inspiring — which attracted the Basic Self's attention and support. In another story Michael described a young girl named Wilma Rudolph, who had contracted polio as a child and walked with a leg brace, and went on to glory as a world-record holding Olympic champion sprinter, undercutting any excuses his listeners might have entertained. Wilma Rudolph's story was true. As to Michael's personal stories? Well, they were typically instructive metaphors, whether literally true or not.

One practical method for working directly with the Basic Self involved freeing myself from the so-called god of opinion (so I could better connect with the god of my heart, or inner knower). Michael instructed me to build a small altar and place my own little god of opinion there. Each morning for the next few weeks, I was to get on my knees and bow down to this little god, saying aloud such things as "I worship you, oh god of opinion. Do I look okay? Do you approve of what I'm doing?" This silly little ceremony brought a subconscious tendency into the light of awareness, helping me to get over my overconcern with other people's opinions. He suggested I name my little god of opinion Wuddle, as in "Wuddle they think? Wuddle they say?"

Another deceptively simple exercise broke the bad habit of berating myself for perceived screwups. Whenever I was down about myself, he told me to put on a pair of those Groucho Marx glasses with the huge nose, mustache, and furry eyebrows, look at myself in a mirror, and say every terrible thing I could think of about myself while wearing those glasses (or any other silly disguise) to see the ridiculous nature of self-disparagement.

Both these exercises involve humor, loved by children (and the Basic Self). Such techniques had an immediate, practical impact that helped me understand the power of the Basic Self and how it operates. I recall thinking at the time, *This is the kind of practical material I'd like to teach.*

The Basic Self (inner child) is both suggestible and powerful, so its faith may aid bodily healing in ways that deserve further research. This knowledge also helped me understand how hypnosis works, and why most faith and energy healers, homeopathy practitioners, acupuncturists, chiropractors, and other health professionals, including physicians, rely to some degree on the placebo effect to supplement and enhance any sort of treatment by reducing stress, tension, and pain, which improves circulation to accelerate healing.

If the Warrior-Priest was in some sense a merchant of ideas and a charismatic trickster, he behaved in a nonexploitative way in service of others. His guidance in working with and integrating the three selves served as a cosmic instruction manual for the human bodymind in daily life. Several years later, this material would inspire me to begin writing again.

A Sense of Drama

At the Warrior-Priest's rental home in Mill Valley, as part of his confidence work (for the Basic Self), Michael first showed me how to disassemble and reassemble a Glock 9-millimeter pistol and an AK-47 rifle, then challenged me to do this task more quickly, the way some soldiers practice. Prior to this training session, other than my childhood BB-gun days, I had not even held a handgun, much less a semiautomatic weapon. While not really a fan of big guns, I had to admit that handling these formidable weapons did provide a sense of gut-level confidence that I hadn't experienced for years. Now I could understand why gun enthusiasts, who might feel less powerful in other areas of their lives, might enjoy collecting and shooting these powerful firearms.

The following week, I experienced a similar jump in personal power as I learned auto-racing techniques of steering, acceleration, and deceleration, followed by a visit to a local raceway, where I deliberately lost and then recovered control on skid pads. Much of the excitement in these activities was due to Michael's dramatic persona. He made these exercises feel more like preparing for a hostage rescue or body-guarding operation than standard driving instruction.

A Personal Relationship

Within a month of our first meeting, the Warrior-Priest took me to dinner at an upscale restaurant in Larkspur. After a relaxed conversation and an excellent meal, he asked the waiter to bring the dessert sampler tray with an array of nine or ten pricey pastries. Michael said, "We'll take it."

"Take what?" asked the waiter.

"All of it," said the Warrior-Priest with a wave of his hand. We enjoyed a tasty bite of each dessert. Michael's dramatic, unpredictable style reflected the crazy excesses of the mid-1980s; he had a way of making the recipient of his attention feel special, a spiritual seduction of the Basic Self. (I saw him treat John, Karen, A. C., Joy, and others in a similar fashion.)

After dinner, Michael told me, "Later tonight, when you're sleeping, I'm going to send you a message. As soon as you awaken tomorrow morning, note down whatever symbols or ideas you can recall." It felt like an exciting challenge to test any innate ability I might have in dream consciousness.

The next day I told Michael that I couldn't recall any messages or symbols but related the snippet of an odd dream. He just shrugged it off, saying it was no big deal. I was disappointed at having failed this test. At the same time, he could have told me that my dream meant I'd received the message, but he didn't. It spoke to a certain integrity, as well as my lack of talent as a dream traveler, at least on that occasion.

Metaphysical Teachings and Cautions

"The mind is like a parachute; it works best when open," Michael reminded me. And so I maintained an open mind and agnostic disposition related to his more speculative teachings. Metaphysical folks seemed to have their own language and interpretation of the world. One person might catch a cold, while another interprets it as a "cleansing crisis."

Since the Warrior-Priest demonstrated clear expertise in and original insights into the martial arts, I was willing to give him the benefit of the doubt even when he gave seminars on out-of-body travel, absent healing, and entities and possession. In this latter talk, he described how certain individuals became vulnerable to "influence by subtle entities in the etheric dimension due to rips in the aura" from overuse of alcohol and other drugs. He also spoke of angels and master healers and guides that we meet in the dream state. I found such information intriguing, though it wasn't something I'd personally experienced and therefore had no intention of teaching.

On other occasions, Michael's metaphysical notions had practical applications in everyday life. For example, the Flame Meditation was based on the idea that negative thoughts appear as dark spots floating in human aura or bioenergy field. If I was troubled by unpleasant thoughts, I could clear these thought-forms from my field of awareness by gazing into a candle flame, letting it dissolve the dark spots up into the ethers. As with most of his techniques, it seemed to work. (Haven't we all enjoyed a relaxed state of reverie while gazing into the flames of a fireplace or campfire?)

Another internal practice, which Michael called The Spiritual Senses, involved connecting my voice (or touch, or even thoughts) to my heart. He explained, "If you place two well-tuned guitars next to one another and pluck any string of one guitar, the corresponding string on the other guitar will also vibrate — an example of sympathetic or harmonic resonance. The same principle works with the human voice: If you speak from your mind, it resonates with the mind of the other person. If you speak from your heart, that resonates with the heart of the other person." All I had to do was to put my attention in my heart when I spoke (or made physical contact). I could even connect my heart to thoughts such as *I love you*, *I support you*, *God bless you*, and so on. When upset, I found that this simple act could lead to emotional healing and a deeper connection between people.

The Warrior-Priest also taught techniques such as tapping or thumping on the chest, directly over the thymus gland (just below the sternum or breastbone) to provide extra energy when needed and to stimulate the immune system — another simple practice I could seamlessly use in everyday life.

Colleagues in Spirit

A couple of months after we met, Michael and I drove across the bay to Berkeley's KPFA radio station around midnight and gave an off-the-wall interview for night owls. Soon after that, he invited me to coteach with him at a workshop he was giving for a group of psychotherapists in a location he vaguely referred to as "somewhere north of Santa Cruz, California." As we were about to drive past San Francisco International Airport, Michael suddenly took the airport exit. It turned out we were flying to Alaska.

Once on the plane, I discovered in my seat pocket a black-and-red Search & Rescue T-shirt like the one Michael wore, and a nylon auto-racing-style jacket. He'd also given me a small handheld recorder for making notes to myself — not a big deal in today's age of smartphones, but back in 1985 it was cutting-edge cool and quite practical.

As we flew into the night, Michael handed me a special *hemi-synch* cassette, whose recorded sound, he claimed, would give me at least four hours' worth of sleep in ninety minutes. "Handy when traveling," he said. I must have fallen asleep at some point but awoke in the night reflecting on the changes in me since meeting the Warrior-Priest.

Self-respect had come easily during my days as a college athlete, coach, and college professor. But by the late 1970s, I'd lost the scent of a career path even as my college teammates earned advanced degrees in medicine, physics, or the law, or entered the financial sector and then went on to thriving professions. After my faculty days at Oberlin ended, my identity floundered. I was a seeker of wisdom with no steady means of support. (My friends sometimes asked, "Hey, Dan, what are you doing *this* week?")

As Michael had said, "Some people make things happen, some watch what happens, and others wonder what happened." In the early 1980s I had watched and wondered, considering a failed first marriage followed by two failed books. And just a few months before I met Michael, Joy and I were invited up to the Guru's sanctuary. I accepted out of curiosity, to see if there were any sparks left. (There weren't.) During our guided tour, I ran into one of the Guru's longtime devotees in charge of purchasing books for the library. Having seen a then out-of-print hardback copy of *Way of the Peaceful Warrior*, he remarked, "Ah, so now you're now a guru, too, Millman?" — implying that in writing a book, I no longer knew my proper place in the community hierarchy, where the only appropriate relationship was humble submission.

Then along came Michael Bookbinder, the Warrior-Priest, who described himself as a cheerleader to the soul just when my soul needed some cheering.

In the morning, before we landed in Alaska, Michael made two unusual predictions: first, that our time together would be relatively brief, and second, that he'd foreseen the circumstances of his death, but not the time. He wouldn't elaborate about either one.

When we arrived in Juneau, he rented a car and showed me

around, pointing out typical Alaskan homes with one or two cars up on blocks in the front yards during this brief summer season, and making a special point to show me a resort area called Alyeska.

Later that day, from the hotel phone, I called Joy and let her know that I was enjoying a cool evening north of Santa Cruz, before telling her just how far north.

Since the group of psychologists in Juneau were fans of Michael Bookbinder, he'd do nearly all the teaching; I was there as an apprentice. But I did introduce a flowing, four-minute workout (derived from my background in dance, gymnastics, martial arts, yoga, and the Arica movements), which I called the Peaceful Warrior Workout, a routine that I'd perform daily and teach for decades.

Fresh Start

Meanwhile, as my word-of-mouth readership continued to expand, speaking invitations began to arrive in the mail. Though I wasn't well-known enough to fill an auditorium, I could draw ten to twenty readers for a weekend workshop. People from small towns across America volunteered to host a weekend event in their home or a rented space at a local school or bookstore. They did local marketing, putting up flyers, inserting bookmarks into copies of my books at local bookshops, and handling registrations. For their efforts, I covered their expenses and gave them a few hundred dollars plus two or three free slots in the workshop.

The content of these early workshops featured principles and practices I'd drawn together from gymnastics and martial arts, as well as big-picture perspectives adapted from the Professor, the Guru, and the Warrior-Priest, especially work with the three selves. Inspired by a flood of new insights, I presented a workshop near our home.

Michael's gift to me went beyond content. He also served as a role model whose words and gestures reached not only attendees' Conscious Selves, but also their Basic and Higher Selves, multiplying the impact and spiritual authority of my words. In this way, my association with the Warrior-Priest prompted a new approach to my teaching.

But an unseen problem surfaced: At the conclusion of my first workshop, my publisher and friend Hal Kramer drew me aside. "Dan, you've said repeatedly, 'Michael taught me this,' and, 'according to Michael Bookbinder' — stop citing this Bookbinder fellow! It's good to acknowledge your teachers, but the people attending your workshop have read *Way of the Peaceful Warrior* and they've come to listen to what *you* have to say. It's now a part of your teaching, so speak from your own authority, not someone else's." It was valuable advice that I took to heart. It forced me to step into my own shoes.

In the months that followed, I sorted and adapted the martial arts elements I'd learned, including board breaking, the Cosmic Stance, and the Unbendable Arm. I also presented the three selves and taught the Peaceful Warrior Workout. I spoke in my own words about how and why it serves us to focus on the present moment, and outlined the benefits and myths of meditation. The key question was always: *What can I share in the amount of time we have that's directly relevant to people's everyday lives?*

Then a small publisher in Vermont offered to republish my first book, *Whole Body Fitness*, under a new title, *The Warrior Athlete*, to capitalize on the warrior theme. Soon I recorded a second talk, then a third, and more recordings on a variety of topics. These audio programs and the workout video marked the beginning of the business that Joy and I named Peaceful Warrior Services.

A Persona Shift

After our trip to Alaska, I grew a short, dark beard like Michael's. That wasn't unusual. I'd periodically let my beard grow — but now, on those occasions when Michael and I both wore black martial arts pants and black Search & Rescue T-shirts and white sneakers, we looked like fraternal twins. I'd affixed the round, magnetic Search & Rescue logos he'd given me on the doors of my vintage Honda, turning it into an official-looking staff car. (I've kept one magnetic logo all these years as a memento.)

At a local evening talk Michael gave in San Rafael, the room was packed with people I recognized, including some core members of the Guru's community. The Warrior-Priest's aura of mystery, adventure, and even danger served as an irresistible attraction to spiritual aspirants in the Bay Area. Given my formerly invisible, worker-bee status in the community, I was pleased to see their surprised faces when the Warrior-Priest introduced me as an integral member of the Search & Rescue staff.

As long as I could remember, I'd sought to improve myself through martial arts and gymnastics, memory and speed-reading courses, expanding my vocabulary with *Word Power Made Easy*, even dabbling in the Trachtenberg system of speed mathematics. I'd learned to juggle, perform sleight-of-hand magic, and play a few songs on the guitar.

Now, my time with the Warrior-Priest marked a fundamental shift. I realized that no matter how much I improved myself, only one person benefited, but if I could help improve the lives of other people, that added meaning to my own life. It was time to "stand up inside myself," as the Warrior-Priest had put it.

Sudden Self-Knowledge

My evolving relationship with the Warrior-Priest felt like a race car going from zero to ninety in the space of a few seconds. Everything kicked into high gear the morning he invited me once again to his home in the hills of Mill Valley.

In my ongoing quest for insight, I'd studied biorhythms, the Lüscher color test, the Myers-Briggs personality test based on Jungian archetypes, and the MMPI or Minnesota Multiphasic Personality Inventory, as well as oracles such as the I-Ching, Tarot, and Nordic runes; I'd looked at astrology from a distance, and studied many maps, models, and teachings from the Professor and the Guru.

I was also aware of the cold-read methods used by so-called psychics, spirit mediums, fortune-tellers, and con artists, who offered vague or general information that their clients might interpret as meaningful, then asked leading questions to glean more information.

Then came the Life Purpose System. As soon as I arrived, Michael said, "I'm going to share some information with you about your life path and destiny." As we sat with eyes closed, the Warrior-Priest began with a sacred invocation he termed "calling on the light." Then he shared a story he said was one of my past lives from the sixteenth century. The idea of reincarnation is a part of both Hindu and Buddhist cosmologies, and embraced by many. If I accepted this idea of past and future lives, it would help to explain certain phenomena, such as resonance with (or antipathy for) a particular locale or culture that I'd never visited (this lifetime, at least), or even that feeling of recognition when I'd met Joy and other key people in my life.

Whether Michael's rendition of my past life was genuine or metaphorical, the story felt both true and moving for reasons I'd later understand. It wasn't a happy story but an instructive one, pointing out one reason my soul was back again to do it right (or at least better) this time.

The Warrior-Priest then described latent qualities I possessed that were waiting to emerge, as well as hurdles I was here to overcome, all of which hit home. I was mystified by how he could illuminate a life path I'd been tripping over in the dark all these years. Michael Bookbinder seemed to understand my life path better than I did — until now.

I remember asking him, "Do you have psychic abilities?"

"Not really," he replied. "Most psychics don't even have psychic abilities. But I've been trained to know where to look." He offered no further explanation, but that phrase stayed with me. Armed with clarity about my innate drive to influence others, I set out to learn how to do just that.

The Search & Rescue Instructor Training

I was fascinated with the Warrior-Priest's method of knowing where to look. So when he announced a four-week advanced training on the Hawaiian island of Maui, I jumped at the chance, again feeling that sense of certainty, of destiny. He would teach, among other things, the system that gave him such uncanny insight into people's lives via the life-path reading, which might enable me to do for other people what he'd done for me.

Joy and I made arrangements to travel to Maui, bringing along a trusted acquaintance to care for our young daughters while we were in class sessions. On arrival, we met fourteen other participants excited about the array of advanced teachings.

Each morning I led the group through the Peaceful Warrior Workout. After that, we spent the bulk of each morning practicing basic movements of Filipino knife fighting (*kali-escrima-arnis*) to prepare ourselves for what the Warrior-Priest called a graduation ceremony near the end of the training. In the afternoons, we learned other techniques of massage and healing. We also practiced shadowboxing to music, wrapping our hands like boxers while being timed, and other elements to enhance inner strength and confidence.

John had already taught the knife-fighting Confidence Training with Michael, so he served as chief assistant instructor, along with A.C. They circulated among us each day, encouraging and correcting. This wasn't the sober atmosphere of many martial arts schools, but a "Shaolin temple with a sense of humor," as Michael put it, pulling a rubber chicken out of his supply bag with a dramatic flourish. He explained, "As you learn to move off the line of attack, block properly, and counter, you're going to make mistakes. That's fine. Your instructors will offer corrections. But do not repeat the *same* mistake twice. If you do, you'll meet…the rubber chicken!" He demonstrated by walking up to me as if to correct my stance. The rubber chicken's long neck and head suddenly swiveled, pointing to my foot.

These lighthearted methods were also serious, because they worked. Whenever anyone noticed Michael or John picking up that chicken, everyone made frantic corrections in their form.

Sometimes we drilled in silence, other times to music. We practiced attacks and defenses, as relaxed as possible and moving slowly, as in tai chi, until the skills transferred from the brain's prefrontal lobe to a more instinctual region — what the Warrior-Priest referred to as cell-level memory — as the moves became automatic.

Each morning Michael spoke about martial arts and life. He put us on notice that to "survive" the coming test, we'd have to respond instinctively. "In combat, as in life, if you start thinking too much, you're dead. We work with knives because many of you have been cut or killed in previous incarnations. We could do the same moves unarmed, but working with the knife provides a focus and gets your full attention. Your Basic Selves take the knife seriously."

He got that right.

At one point, the Warrior-Priest described how, during teaching visits to state and federal prisons — work that reflected his Search & Rescue ethos — he established his credibility among the muscular, tattooed inmates by asking for a volunteer to stand and face him. Michael then took a martial arts stance, looked at the man, and in a few seconds, he somehow caused the man's knees to buckle from across the room.

When asked how he did it, he answered, "I let *his* Basic Self see *my* Basic Self" (which, we assumed, was powerful). When someone asked if he'd demonstrate this feat, he shook his head. "I stopped doing that demonstration after one of the inmate volunteers had a seizure."

At this point no one, including me, was ready to volunteer until the Warrior-Priest agreed to give a modified demonstration that would only temporarily weaken a volunteer rather than collapse him. Bob volunteered, and Joe, a chiropractor in our group, agreed to test Bob's strength before and after.

Both Bob and Joe confirmed that he felt weaker afterward, demonstrating either Michael's ability or the power of suggestion.

Surviving the Knife Test

As the upcoming knife test drew near, practice suddenly got very real. Recalling how I'd told my Stanford gymnastics team about the low and high balance beams, I treated every practice session like the final test.

Then time sped up as the Warrior-Priest announced the test on the following morning. "You'll sit around the perimeter of the room. When called, each of you will stand in the center, facing me. After we bow in, I'll attack each of you numerous times with this knife" — he displayed a dulled steel training knife instead of the rubber ones we'd all used in practice. "Those who show grace under pressure will pass the test. Those who don't will fail. And for anyone who fails the test, this training is over."

A chill of anxiety seemed to pervade the entire group. The Warrior-Priest hadn't yet revealed his method for seeing people's life paths. I wondered, *Will anyone who fails the knife test miss this critical information?*

The next morning, we filed into the space and sat around the room. My mouth was dry and cottony; the sensation was even more intense than in my competition days. This wasn't about performing a routine but about facing the Warrior-Priest, who entered as relaxed as ever. He began with a few words I'll paraphrase: "This test isn't just about knife-fighting skill, but about how you face your doubt, your insecurity, your fear. The question you'll answer with your body is this: Can you make the necessary shift to not only pass the test but to live more fully?"

The Warrior-Priest continued: "If you aren't yet ready to make this leap of faith in yourself, you'll fail the test. Those who fail inevitably learn twice as much as those who pass. Nonetheless," he repeated, "if you fail, this training is over. It's not up to me; it's up to you. I'm just a mirror of how you face the challenges of your life."

As my fellow students and I sat with nervous alertness, Michael concluded: "I'll begin with one or two smooth, slow attacks, running past you to your left or right with a slash, as you've practiced, or I may run directly at you with a knife thrust to your throat or abdomen. After the first few attacks, I'm going to speed up and test your limits. Remember, the only difference between fear and excitement is whether you're breathing. Trust yourself and your training. I wish you well."

I felt the adrenaline pumping through my bloodstream as the Warrior-Priest called Joy forward. I watched in rapt attention as he indicated for her to stand about ten feet away and face him. They each bowed while keeping eyes on each other as he'd instructed us. He stood poised, then sprinted toward her, lunging, cutting —

Joy sidestepped, fended off the knife arm, and sliced at his arm with her rubber knife. He turned, then came in faster, just as he'd predicted. Joy moved in response, just as she'd practiced. Again and again. Then it was over. He gestured for her to bow out with him. Then he said, "You pass."

Joy sat down next to me, glowing, still breathing with exertion. After a hand squeeze, she turned, ready to observe and support her classmates. If I were to guess about the thoughts now floating around the training room, they would have been something like: *It can be done. It's not impossible. But what if I fall apart or freeze up?*

In my case, falling apart wasn't an issue. I had a long history of grace under pressure. But hubris might be my undoing, and I sensed that Michael knew this. All my past reluctance to spar with someone attacking me came to the fore. *Would this be my downfall?*

The next person lost their composure and failed. My stomach clenched. A dark cloud seemed to settle over the room. Finally, when my name was called, I sensed that Michael might give me a hard time.

In the end, it felt like stepping into a time warp. I evaded and fended off not only his attacks but my own internal narrative about how I could be or should be doing better. Then we bowed out, and he said, "You pass."

Wait a minute, I thought, *is it over already? Did he go easy on me?* Others followed. Most passed. Two more failed.

The Warrior-Priest said, "In everyday life people learn tough lessons: car crashes, cancer. Life doesn't give second chances. But this training has been a padded place to learn about yourself. So I offer those of you who failed the opportunity to test again if you're willing to call forth whatever resources you need to break through whatever's been holding you back."

Of the three people who chose to request a second test, two of them passed and one failed a second time. As soon as that individual returned to his seat, the Warrior-Priest said to him, "You did the best you could at this time. But as I said before, this training is over for you."

A melancholy quiet filled the room during a long pause before Michael spoke again: "I now declare this training over. Today, right now, we begin a new training for the final three days." He turned to the person who had failed, and said, "Welcome back."

Now I viewed the knife training as an initiation for what was about to follow.

Joy's Memories

I remember the knife test. It was fast and scary. When it was over, I breathed a sigh of relief. Not having previously studied any martial arts, even after all the hours of practice I found it challenging to demonstrate the flowing, relaxed movement necessary to pass the test. It didn't require anyone to be a top athlete, so it was accessible to most people. More than anything, it was a test of courage, which is why Dan ended up calling it the Peaceful Warrior Courage Training for all the years he later taught his version of the course.

Life Purpose Revelations

That evening, when I entered the seminar room and looked around, I could feel the excitement. The moment had finally arrived when the Warrior-Priest would reveal the system that had provided each of us with a clear sense of purpose and might enable us to do the same for others.

Michael began with the words: "When you were born, your parents gave you a name and the universe gave you a number or frequency related to your date of birth…"

This sounds like numerology, I thought — an occult art that had never appealed to me, since it made no sense how adding up all the numbers of a person's date of birth could uncover valid information about core elements of that individual's life. Yet everyone in the room could testify to the revelations that brought us here.

Michael went on to explain, "Many cultures have evolved numerological systems according to their ancient calendars. Even using the more accurate Gregorian calendar today, different systems add and interpret the numbers in different ways. As you've noticed," he said, "I've found a more accurate interpretation." I saw nods of agreement around the room.

The Warrior-Priest then began a lecture that would continue for the next two evenings, sharing his method of deriving insights into anyone's life. I took careful notes of his lectures, typing and organizing my scribbled notes the way I'd done back in college. It felt crucial for me to study this information while it was fresh.

Each evening he shared highlights about the meaning of all the combined birth numbers — calculated by adding together all the digits in a person's date of birth — pinpointing key issues for each of thirty-seven life paths (which expanded to forty-five after the year 2000). Now I understood how the Warrior-Priest had used the life-path information to create a resonant past-life scenario mirroring issues we'd each encountered on our respective life paths.

Meanwhile, I'd already begun memorizing my notes, twenty pages in all, anticipating readings that I'd offer to friends, relatives, and eventually to paying clients. Reflecting on what the Warrior-Priest had revealed, I knew it couldn't be proved or explained any more than we could derive the square root of a sonnet. It wasn't a science, after all, but an artful system or lens to bring aspects of life into focus.

I thought about a quip I'd once heard about how "people make fun of astrologers and numerologists yet believe the predictions of economists." I thought it odd how many people were so ready to accept elegant but unproven theories like Jung's *anima* and *animus*; Freud's ego, superego, and id; the Myers-Briggs psychological inventory; or physicists' cosmic but unproven hypotheses like string theory or the Big Bang.

What Michael had revealed might not be provable or even explainable, but I had no doubts about its utility. That life-purpose reading he had provided had enabled me to step more fully into my current teaching role, now armed with new tools to serve others.

In his final lecture, Michael summarized certain spiritual laws (or universal principles) that clients could apply to overcome the hurdles on their respective life paths. In closing, he cautioned us against simply painting by numbers in a rote fashion, and encouraged us to share impressions that came up during the session. When I later offered Spiritual Law Alignment readings, I was sometimes surprised by the content that appeared.

During an open discussion, I said, "Michael, the Law of Balance suggests that for every strength is a corresponding weakness. We've seen your strengths. Can you share something about your weaknesses?" Michael only came up with: "I can be a badass at times, as some of you know." I heard some chuckles in the room, but he'd dodged the question. That's when it struck me that our true flaws are the ones that remain hidden, even to ourselves. If someone asks me about my own flaws, the most honest response I can give is, "You'll have to ask Joy."

Crisis

On the final morning of the training, a tragic incident occurred that would set in motion a series of events that, like falling dominoes, would change my relationship with the Warrior-Priest, the course of his future, and the course of my own as well.

It began with an image seared into my memory: Joy and I, with our little daughters and babysitter, were eating breakfast when John burst out of the nearby training room door carrying the limp figure of the Warrior-Priest in his arms. I followed John, Karen, and a few others into Michael's room. Joe the chiropractor attended until emergency medical help arrived and transported Michael to a hospital. We spent the rest of that afternoon in a daze, processing what had occurred.

That final evening, with everyone packed to fly back home the next day, John gathered the group and explained that Michael had suffered a brain bleed due to a congenital arteriovenous malformation (AVM). He had a good chance of survival, but with a temporary speech impairment and paralysis on one side of his body.

On that sad note, a diaspora began. We said our farewells before dispersing around the United States, Canada, and overseas. After flying home, Joy and I caught up as our girls started a new school. I had several upcoming workshops and writing projects in the works.

I later learned that after Michael was airlifted back to his Mill Valley house, he received physical and occupational therapy and home care. Due to the location of the bleed, surgery was deemed too risky. John and Karen moved in to support him in any way they could. I stayed in touch with John for status updates. The Warrior-Priest was not accepting any visitors while he focused on the hard road back. If anyone could regain mobility and improved speech, he could.

On-the-Job Training

After studying and contemplating my twenty pages of notes on the life-path material, I contacted local friends and relatives, offering a free life-purpose consultation. Referring to my notes, I began with a few introductory remarks — then, after calling on the light, I shared what I could.

Within a few weeks I'd internalized all the information and no longer needed any notes. As my confidence and capacity grew, I started charging a fee for the service. Whenever I traveled to give a talk or workshop, I scheduled time to fit in a few in-person readings.

Then, a month after the Maui training, John asked if I'd volunteer to help him teach a five-day knife training that the Warrior-Priest had committed to before getting sidelined. All income beyond our travel went to Michael's care. A. C. and Karen also assisted. It was an intense and positive experience being on the teaching side of this transformative work, and a chance to learn by doing. I also helped John with the testing, gauging how fast and assertive I could be to stretch the limits of each student. We consulted with each other before declaring a pass or fail.

I was so impressed with the insights and shifts participants reported that I resolved to contact all those on my postal mailing list and update our brochure to include a description of the

Peaceful Warrior Courage Training, which, given my physical background, I now felt confident to teach.

The first such knife training took place on three weekday evenings, then one full weekend in a multipurpose room of a former school. The twelve participants, some local and a few from across the country, experienced significant shifts, and several of them became lifelong friends. One woman, who didn't seem engaged and even missed one of the training sessions, returned the next day, caught up, and passed her test; a week later she sent me a monetary bonus because the training had meant so much to her. Another participant, a physician from the Netherlands, struggled with coordination through most of the training until one evening he turned to me, his eyes wide with wonder, and declared, "I can feel my legs!" He'd finally connected to the earth. Despite passing his test a few days later, that grounding moment during practice may have been his biggest takeaway, his *kensho* moment.

In a later Courage Training, a couple from the UK sent me a postcard after their return home, contributing a poetic summary of their experience: "The thrusting knife teaches trusting life." Leave it to the Brits to come up with the right turn of phrase.

When one of the trainees asked whether I was a pacifist, I answered, "Yes and no," pointing out that the most extreme practitioners of nonviolence become fruitarians, eating only fruit that falls from the trees to avoid killing, say, a carrot. Yet even fruitarians kill millions of bacteria each time they breathe. "Absolute harmlessness is not possible," I said, "which is why I practice relative pacifism." If I'd decided to avoid self-defense training because it was too violent, that choice wouldn't make me a pacifist, but it might make me a victim. *Since no one has a right to attack or injure me*, I thought, *when I defend myself by disabling the attacker, I provide a consequence for their behavior. So I practice relative pacifism while respecting my body and boundaries.* I told my groups,

"Learning self-defense needs no justification. In fact, it seems a responsibility and an essential life skill."

I would offer the Courage Training three or four times a year for fourteen years, each class filled to capacity. Participants came from all over the world. Most had no martial arts experience, but we drew a few high-ranking black belts curious about the process.

New Role, New Circumstance

The Warrior-Priest's disabilities would have been a tough burden for anyone to bear, but far worse for him, a once-fit adventurer who valued his independence and easygoing style. When I was finally invited to visit him, he was still in a wheelchair, looking thin, even frail. John had helped him into his auto-racing nylon jacket, striped martial arts pants, and something new: a black beret with numerous pins on it that Michael said he received for his contribution in special ops. Seeing all these totems broke my heart, and I think he knew it.

I began sending Michael a percentage of my income from workshops, seminars, and Spiritual Law Alignment readings to help with his rent and maintenance needs during this transition period. Thanks in large part to what I'd learned from the Warrior-Priest, our income was improving, and he had offered Joy and me trainings at no charge.

I now had new tools and perspectives and was carrying selected aspects of his work out into the world, especially the Courage Training and life-path material. So helping him financially seemed both appropriate and responsible. Scrapper-survivor that he was, the Warrior-Priest also managed to produce income of his own, with telephone readings and an occasional evening seminar; I helped to promote some of his services and occasionally assisted as support staff.

Michael sold health-related products, such as "pulsars" that he claimed users could wear to counterbalance "potentially damaging EMF radiation" from computer screens. He also sold brain-synching cassette recordings designed to deepen meditation and "tune and balance" the brain hemispheres. I later learned that these recent brain-synch tapes were recordings of his vacuum cleaner. When I asked Michael about this, he deflected the question with typical humor, saying, "After listening, most clients report feeling cleaner."

As the months passed, my teaching work and family responsibilities led me and Michael into parallel lives. Previously latent aspects of his personality, which may have been there all along, grew exaggerated after the profound and debilitating disruption he'd experienced. In researching AV malformations, I learned that jazz guitarist Pat Martino had developed amnesia and bipolar symptoms after suffering a brain bleed, which might help explain the growing paranoia and other personality changes I noticed in the Warrior-Priest.

A few weeks later, I learned that with John's and Karen's help, Michael had put most of his possessions in storage and had moved down to Southern California into a spare room of one of his most devoted clients and supporters.

That winter of 1986, Joy and I had saved enough money, supplemented by loans from our families, for a down payment on our first home in San Rafael, where we and our growing daughters would live for decades to come. After living on a shoestring budget for years, we finally had a regular income stream. My talks and workshops opened the way for a new career aligned with my longtime calling as a teacher.

The increasing interest in my work meant more frequent time away from home. Soon I was away for two or three weekends a month. My time away from home was a sacrifice for me and for my family. Once, when I called home, after I spoke with Joy and then Sierra, Joy put the phone to three-year-old China's ear. She said, "Are you my daddy?" When I said yes, Joy told me that China lovingly petted the phone receiver.

Even when I was home, my intensive focus on my work left me with less attention than I might have given to my daughters, leaving it to Joy to make up for my lacks, which she did admirably. But during their teenage years, I realized that my relative lack of involvement with the day-to-day lives of my daughters affected our relationships. I don't want to exaggerate my absences — I dearly loved my daughters, and they knew it. But they also knew that I'd chosen to focus on my work over the less defined, some-times more chaotic, duties of family, where I sometimes floun-dered.

Yet, for the first time, I had a sense that I might earn a decent living, supporting my family while doing what life had prepared me to do. The impact of Michael Bookbinder's work had enlivened my career and my life. And it couldn't have come at a better time.

I thought back to that Thursday evening the previous year when Joy had encouraged me to attend the introductory talk by the Warrior-Priest. But for her comment, he and I might never have met.

Parting of the Ways

All my adventures with the Warrior-Priest had unfolded in the space of two years — a period of radical change for both of us. As Michael himself had said, "Sometimes you get the elevator, and sometimes you get the shaft."

In the late spring of 1988 Michael called to ask if I'd be will-ing to rent a van, get his things out of storage, drive them down to Southern California, and drop them off at the home where he was now staying. "Sure," I said before he added, "If you can stick around here for a few days, feel free to attend a weekend workshop I'm teaching on out-of-body travel." I said I'd have to check my schedule, but in any case I'd inform my mailing list about his workshop.

It turned out I had a family commitment on that Sunday. I arrived late Friday afternoon and unloaded Michael's possessions. Then, having booked a hotel for only one night since I had to fly home the next morning, I dropped by the workshop in time to hear Michael's typically enticing introduction. He described various platforms of awareness and how, through a particular kind of meditation, we could access ever-higher platforms to the point of noncorporeal awareness. He would teach this approach the following day.

I nodded to a few old friends whom I'd informed about the training, including Judy, who'd assisted me in several Courage Trainings. Then, during a break, Michael invited me to join him for a few minutes in his room. I told him how glad I was to see him, then mentioned that his belongings were in the garage, and that due to a family commitment I had to fly home in the morning. He gave me a hug and said, "It's good to see you again, brother."

Although I didn't know it, we would never meet again.

As his evening seminar reconvened, I drove to my hotel room near the airport. An hour or two later, before I drifted off to sleep, Joy called my room. She sounded concerned: "Did something happen between you and Michael?"

"No," I said. "What's up?"

"Judy just called to tell me that after you left, at the end of the evening, Michael announced that you're no longer authorized to work with Search & Rescue."

I later called Judy, who confirmed what the Warrior-Priest had said.

I tried unsuccessfully to reach Michael through his host, and reached out to see if John or Karen could lend any insight, but they were no longer in touch with Michael after his move south.

Writings and Trainings

Unable to reach the Warrior-Priest, who had since moved back to Alaska, I turned my attention to new writing projects. Nine years after the initial publication of *Way of the Peaceful Warrior*, I planned to write a small book describing the three selves, but that project transformed into a teaching novel about my meetings with a Hawaiian *kahuna* named Mama Chia in a rain forest on the island of Molokai. I titled it *Sacred Journey of the Peaceful Warrior*. The following year I wrote *No Ordinary Moments*, a peaceful warrior's guide to daily life. I sent both books to Michael. They were returned unopened. He'd cut off all ties with me and with John and Karen, who had taken care of him during his initial recovery.

Meanwhile, my work continued to evolve. In the early 1990s, after teaching the Courage Training for several years, I created two advanced trainings, an array of adventures centered around mortality and courage, with two days in a forest featuring a high ROPES (Repetitive Obstacle Performance Evaluation System) challenge course.

One morning at the first advanced training, I woke all training participants before dawn and handed them driving directions to a small local airport, where we took turns bungee jumping from a hot-air balloon floating three hundred feet above the concrete below (like jumping from a thirty-story building) — another experience in facing our fears. Then, after a thirty-minute preparatory class, we each tried tandem skydiving, leaping from an airplane from twelve thousand feet. Our witty Australian jumpmaster said,

"When the chute opens, if the people below look like ants, that's good, but if the ants look like people, that's bad."

Most of the next day was devoted to Holotropic Breathwork, the closest thing to a drug-free LSD trip via prolonged hyperventilation, combined with powerful music, an experience created by Stanislav and Christina Grof. Participants also wrote their own epitaph, obituary, and memorial speech as a means of considering their eventual death and appreciating life. All of this was intended to deepen and intensify their experience as peaceful warriors in training in the school of life.

During this productive phase of my teaching work, realizing that I could reach only a limited number of people with my Spiritual Law Alignment sessions and audiotapes, I created a seven-day Life Purpose Certification Training for health professionals and life coaches who could make practical use of the life-path information in service of others. Over seven days, I shared all that I'd learned along with emerging insights about life paths, spiritual laws, and related topics. Then the participants practiced giving readings to one another.

Some of their notebooks were so extensive and well organized they resembled book manuscripts. But since no attendee had my depth of experience with the material, I felt an urgent sense of responsibility to write a book revealing all facets of the Life Purpose System for the wider public. Having made this decision, I again tried to contact the Warrior-Priest several times without success.

It took two years of intensive writing before the book was ready for publication. Joy and I brainstormed and struggled with a title until one afternoon when we walked through our living room while our girls were watching *The Sound of Music*. The Mother Superior was saying, "Maria, you have to go out and find the life you were born to live."

Books: Lined Up on the Runway

When *The Life You Were Born to Live* was published in 1994, it attracted a significant readership. Those original twenty pages of notes I'd typed at the Warrior-Priest's advanced training had now expanded into a book of four hundred pages. A key section outlined seventeen different spiritual laws to help overcome the hurdles on particular life paths. (A year later, I decided that these laws were important enough to merit a book of their own, which evolved into a teaching tale I called *The Laws of Spirit*.)

During my author tour for *The Life You Were Born to Live*, I explained that life purpose was only one element of the peaceful warrior's way — one facet of personal growth. Which begged the question: What topics make up the entire arena of personal growth? In response to that question, a list of twelve areas came to me — twelve courses in the school of daily life that would, several years later, form the basis of another major book I would title *Everyday Enlightenment*.

By the summer of 1996, Joy and I and our daughters, now in their teens, all lived busy and productive lives, together as a family yet immersed in our own worlds. Meanwhile, as the circle of *Peaceful Warrior* readers grew, my work expanded across the United States and in various locales overseas.

Joy's Memories

The next couple of decades were Dan's writing and teaching years. I spent my time raising our daughters (with his help, to be sure) and reading manuscripts, discussing the trainings with him, answering letters, doing bookkeeping, and managing our office after we hired someone else to help. I also did volunteer work in our daughters' middle and high schools.

During that period I occasionally looked back on our years with the various teachers. Were we naïve, easily influenced? I don't think so. Dan and I, in our own ways, were searching for the best way to live, to be in the world, to be helpful. Neither of us was comfortable surrendering our whole selves to someone else's path. As I mentioned earlier, we mostly stayed on the periphery except with Michael, who didn't require such a deep level of commitment.

After our experiences together in these various groups, I now understood the difference between learning from teachers and being controlled by them.

A Dialogue with Socrates

So you had quite a wild ride with that Bookbinder fellow, Soc chimed in, as if we'd just been carrying on a conversation.

Now quicker on the uptake, I asked, "You think it was predestined?"

In retrospect, everything seems predestined.

"Well, it was quite the roller coaster; never a dull moment with the Warrior-Priest."

Looking back on that time, what do you think of him?

"The Warrior-Priest was a spiritual placebo artist, a brilliant teacher, a seller of ideas."

I take it that you had less interest in his more — what did you call them? — speculative ideas.

"Yeah, the metaphysical stuff. Well, there's physics, which covers the smallest quantum particle to the cosmos. Then there's metaphysics — a different way of looking at reality..."

So you did all the Arica work, then hung out with the Guru for —

"Nearly eight years. On and off."

Then the Warrior-Priest entered your life — a spiritual tough guy who helped you get a handle on your life path and purpose, which you desperately needed.

"Bizarre but true. As you know."

What if you'd met them in a different order — say, the Guru first, then the Professor —

"I don't think it would have made sense, because in some fundamental way, each mentor prepared me for the next....Anyway, it happened the way it happened. But if I'd only studied with the Professor, only with Guru, or only with the Warrior-Priest, I might lack the broader perspective that enabled me to write this book."

Clearly, each of them taught far more than the content you've described.

"Absolutely. I couldn't even begin —"

Interesting how you teach only a fraction of what you've learned from the mentors.

"If I parsed everything that I teach today, aiming to find its source, I don't think I could. It's as if each of my mentors helped to unlock a vault of universal truths that came to me, or through me —"

Some people launder money. You launder spiritual teachings.

I had to smile at that. "I'm just glad that some folks like my laundry service. You know, it's a little like downsizing when we moved to a smaller apartment: I had to choose which books to take with me and which to let go of. That's the sorting process I used with the quotations I've collected and with everything I've learned...Socrates? Are you still here?"

A faraway voice: *Always...*

Chapter 12

The Sage

The profound and transcendent
are also found in the factories, the shops.
Such places may not fill you with bliss...
like the spiritual experiences you've read about,
but reality is to be found here, too,
in the way we relate to everyday problems.

CHÖGYAM TRUNGPA

On a lazy Sunday morning in the autumn of 1996, as the Japanese maple outside our window turned scarlet in the morning sun, I sat in our breakfast nook, idly paging through an audio catalogue I'd found in our mail. My eyes were skimming past various programs on mindfulness, wellness, relationships, and self-acceptance when my gaze came to a full stop on a program titled Constructive Living with David K. Reynolds. It described "a way to live well no matter what you're feeling" and how to manage daily life in a simpler, more direct way. It struck me as an honest, grounded presentation without lofty or grandiose claims. Ready for a dose of reality and authenticity, I ordered the Reynolds audio program and, struck by how each mentor had prepared me for the next, I dove into his books.

For decades I'd assumed that spiritual practice necessarily required inner work: fixing or improving my thoughts and feelings, doing spiritual practices, or sitting with an enlightened master in order to live well. Now, from what I'd read, David Reynolds — whom I'll refer to as the Sage — was suggesting an approach independent of thoughts and feelings. His lesson was simple, but my mind remained complicated with maps, models, techniques, and theories. So when I learned of a ten-day residential training just across the bay in San Francisco, I enrolled.

The Sage's Backstory and Teachings

A few months before my fiftieth birthday — *Where had the years gone?* — I showed up on the doorstep of a San Francisco duplex apartment. As a student once again, with a beginner's mind, I hoped for a refreshing change of pace at this Constructive Living Instructor Certification training.

Setting down my suitcase, I pushed the buzzer. The door opened to reveal a man about my height and maybe five years my senior. His hair was cut short, as was his salt-and-pepper beard. "Welcome," he said, picking up my suitcase and carrying it up the stairs. *A polite fellow*, I thought.

At the top of the stairs I asked, "When do I meet David Reynolds?"

"You just did," he answered, reaching out to shake my hand. "I'll let you get settled." His eyes crinkled as he smiled. I decided I liked him.

I shared a cozy basement room with Paul, one of my fellow students. A few minutes later I met Lynn, the Sage's wife, who was also, I soon learned, a schoolteacher and avid tennis player, and one of four other students in the training. Apparently the Sage was accustomed to attracting small groups of nice people.

His opening presentation made the challenges quite clear: There would be morning-to-night study, discussions, tests, various challenges, contemplations, reading, writing, and koan riddles, as well as personal interviews, plus a rigorous final examination. I'd not only have to show a clear understanding of Constructive Living (or CL), I'd have to live it under his watchful eye. The thought arose: *Relax, Dan. You don't have to empty your cup; you just need a bigger cup.*

In his youth David Reynolds was a high achiever: president of the chess club, cocaptain of the junior varsity basketball team, a Bible scholar and justice of the Student Supreme Court. But since there was no college tradition in his family, after high school he joined the Navy as a radio operator stationed in Japan, exposing him to a culture and people who would influence his lifework. After his tour of duty, he attended college, then graduate school, earning a PhD in psychological anthropology from UCLA along with a fellow graduate student and future author named Carlos Castaneda.

During an extended time in Japan as a psychological researcher, the Sage found two primary mentors of his own: a noted psychiatrist named Shōma Morita and a lay Buddhist priest named Ishin Yoshimoto.

Dr. Morita offered a behavior-oriented therapy that helped sensitive people to function well despite complicated and conflicting emotions. His essential message was this: We have little or no control over, and therefore no responsibility for, arising thoughts or ever-changing emotions. But we do have control over our behavior and are responsible for everything we do, no matter what we're feeling.

Morita's approach can be summarized in three steps: First, accept your feelings and thoughts as natural to you in the moment (*accepting*, in this context, means simply noticing, as someone might do in meditation.) Second, choose a constructive purpose or aim. Third, do what needs to be done in line with your chosen purpose — practical advice for functioning well and getting things done. *And*, I thought, *people who get things done are probably going to be more fulfilled and happier than those who don't.*

But since Morita's three guidelines could also help criminals to do their work, the Sage needed a complementary practice to balance Morita's utilitarian therapy. He found that practice in a form of reflection that Yoshimoto called *Naikan*, which means "looking inward." *Naikan* is both a contemplative practice and a moment-to-moment way of seeing ourselves (in relation to other people and the world) that is authentic and three-dimensional.

Naikan reflection is centered around three questions, which I could ask myself at the end of each day in relation to my wife (or anyone else). First: *What have I received from them today?* Second: *What have I given?* Third, and most important: *What troubles or difficulties have I caused them?* According to the Sage, I didn't need to ask the phantom fourth question — *What difficulties have they caused me?* — since, as the Sage stated, "Most of us are already experts at noticing the troubles that others cause us."

David K. Reynolds was the first helping professional to synthesize both Morita's and Yoshimoto's approaches into a single way of life that he aptly named Constructive Living.

Beyond what I've just described, the Sage offered no theories, theology, or abstract conceptual underpinnings — only realistic reminders, which, in his words, "undercut and transcend New Age beliefs, psychodynamic theories, and self-help nostrums."

Constructive Living, I'd later realize, had limited appeal because it wasn't designed to help people feel better; it offered no consolation, only insight. Some people found the Sage's approach off-putting, particularly psychotherapists who were focused instead on getting in touch with feelings, digging through the archaeological detritus of the past, and aiming for an emotional catharsis to heal presumed emotional wounds so patients could feel better about themselves.

"Feelings are important," the Sage explained. "They can provide useful information." (As the Warrior-Priest had put it, "Every emotional charge contains a lesson.") "However," Dr. Reynolds added, "an emotion-centered life is chaotic because feelings and impulses change continually. They need not dominate our lives nor dictate what we do."

In the Sage's Own Words

In a March 1990 *New Dimensions Radio* interview, the Sage gave a personal example of what it means to accept our feelings, then do whatever we need to do:

> I'm afraid to fly. I have a lot of insight about why I'm afraid to fly, but having all that insight has never helped get rid of the fear. I never found a way to feel comfortable with flying. Yet I've flown to Japan twice a year for many years, and to Hawaii and around the United States. Frightened, I fly. What gets me on that plane is my purpose: I need to get to that next lecture. It is not fear that stops people from flying. They don't fly because they don't buy a ticket or walk down the ramp onto the plane and fasten their seat belts.

Listening to this interview, I recalled my own gymnastics training, when I had to "feel the fear and do it anyway" on a daily basis. Since then, however, like many spiritual seekers, I'd invested decades in self-oriented inner work geared toward improving the state of my psyche in order to find fulfillment and peace. The Sage's observations about reality began to undermine such assumptions. He was from the "Just do it" school, reminding us that our lives are shaped not by what we feel or think but most directly by what we do. Which is why Morita once said, "When running up a hill, it's okay to give up [mentally] as many times as you wish, as long as your feet keep moving."

When someone asked the Sage about the fear of public speaking, he said, "At the core of performance anxiety is self-orientation: *Will they like me? Will they hate me? How do I look? Will I mess up and make a fool of myself?* But when self-attention shifts to the task at hand, the experience changes." He then shared advice from Yoshimoto: "When passing by a mirror, notice the frame. Most unhappy people habitually focus on their image in the mirror. Happier people turn their attention to the frame — to other people and the world around them."

After noticing my self-oriented speech patterns, the Sage challenged me to avoid using the word *I* for an entire day. *I* found the task so difficult that *I* got tongue-tied — forcing me to confront the fact that for decades I'd viewed myself as a star surrounded by supporting characters, which worked well for me when I was the little prince of our family and then a gymnastics performer, but hadn't worked as well in my personal relationships.

After all that I'd experienced in life and with my previous three mentors, I could better appreciate the Sage's work. After the Professor's step-by-step process of theory and practice, the Guru's transcendent light seemingly falling into shadow, and the Warrior-Priest's confident role model, which inspired new writing and teaching work, I was ready for the Sage's emphasis on present-oriented, purposeful action as a key to living wisely and well.

Radical Realities

Pushing against common assumptions, like the boy in the story "The Emperor's New Clothes," the Sage pointed out realities that many people, especially neo-Freudian therapists, missed or denied: "There's no such thing as a repressed emotion," he said. "You either feel something or you don't. How can you have an unfelt feeling? Is that like having an unthunk thought?"

The Sage also expressed skepticism about repressed memories seemingly recovered through therapeutic intervention, saying, "Those who have a traumatic experience don't have trouble remembering it; they have trouble forgetting it." (Exceptions include traumatic brain injury or blackouts from alcohol.)

He also suggested that guilt is good for us, noting how guilt can point to a needed action. He gave this example: "A client came to see me to find relief from the guilt he felt due to infrequent visits with his mother in a nearby nursing home. He asked if I could help to reduce or eliminate the guilty feelings that had plagued him. I suggested he visit his mother more often."

And when a New Age journalist asked him about spiritual experiences, the Sage replied:

I had a spiritual experience eating breakfast this morning, another one writing an email, changing clothes...as I think of the efforts of others on my behalf, who support each of those actions, the designers and engineers and farmers and truck drivers and parents of all those [people] and others who enable me to open the refrigerator, sit down to the computer. Everyday miracles. Which would you like to separate out as "spiritual"?

When I asked David how I might cultivate a peaceful state of mind, he replied, "If your house is on fire, an alert, action-oriented mind is more appropriate than a peaceful one. The best attainment is a flexible mind, adapting to changing circumstance."

Real-World Tests

One evening near the end of our residential training, as we all sat around the dinner table finishing our meal, the Sage asked us to close our eyes. He then said, "Please recall the pattern and color of your dinner plate...and the location of lights in this room...and how many mirrors hang on the wall...and where flowers or floral images are visible." He invited us to open our eyes and look at our plate, then around the room. Doing so showed me how reality was more vivid than memory images. The exercise also revealed that while eating and talking, I had paid little attention to my surroundings — how my attention was still largely directed at the mirror of my own mind rather than at the world around me.

The next morning, Dr. Reynolds handed me and each of my fellow students a sheet of paper with an enigmatic riddle that we could solve only by walking around the neighborhood and carefully observing our surroundings, looking for clues he'd referenced in the riddle about a single eye and a green roar. As I walked, looking all around me, I finally spied a moss-covered statue of a weatherworn lion that was missing one eye. Such exercises were designed to draw our attention out of daydreams and ruminations and into the present moment as we noticed the details in our surroundings.

The Sage also gave each of us several different CL koans to test our understanding. Here's one of them: "A student asked me, 'When I truly understand reality, there's no need to read any more of your books, is there?' In the next moment, she ducked a book that came flying her way. Why did I throw the book at her? And how is her ducking the answer to her question?"

One possible answer: Reality happens whether or not the student reads the Sage's books. And she had to respond to each moment, doing whatever needed doing — including ducking.

Although that ten-day training might seem modest compared to my forty days in the first Arica training, or my intensive seven years studying the Guru's teaching, the demands of living constructively served as a reentry into a simple, clear, direct relationship with life as it is.

It was like that old Zen proverb about the beginning, middle, and end of the spiritual journey: "First, mountains are mountains and rivers are rivers; then, after deep insight work, mountains are no longer just mountains, and rivers are no longer mere rivers, but rather profound and meaningful metaphors; finally, at the end of the search, mountains are mountains and rivers are rivers." Everyday life was now my practice and training ground.

The next few weeks after the certification training, I noticed changes in my perspectives and behavior as well as in the emphasis of my teaching work. I found myself noticing, and even embracing, passing thoughts and emotions while focusing on the needs of the moment. Rather than trying to change my subjective mind, I truly understood for the first time that I could function well in the world no matter what thoughts or feelings arose.

Without any effort, daily life became a constant meditation. Noticing. Letting go. Doing what needed to be done. Giving thanks for all the support I constantly received.

Joy's Memories

After reading David's book *Constructive Living*, I had mixed feelings. I appreciated living constructively, but I felt less connection to him or his teaching. Dan and I were already high-functioning people as well as grateful for all the support we'd received from others. Still, when Dan chose to do that residential certification training, I was completely supportive.

I don't think Dan studied Constructive Living as much for his own personal or spiritual development, but more to understand David's approach to reality so it could inform Dan's peaceful warrior work. Constructive Living seemed practical and down-to-earth, but I personally found it obvious. So Dan immersed himself in the CL work on his own.

Pushback on Positive Thinking

In the first seminar I gave after completing the CL training, I found myself, like the Sage, swimming against the current of accepted psychological and New Age notions. After my spiritual quest and ascent into the higher chakras and the sky of mind, it was good to come back to earth and to reality. But now I understood why people weren't flocking to the Sage's work. His approach to living well, while straightforward, wasn't easy.

When people asked me questions like "How can I face my fears...do well on an interview...express myself honestly...get in better shape...earn a decent living...speak in public...write a book...meet new people...keep the house clean...show more discipline?" I'd remind them that they already knew how. Unsatisfied with "Make a good effort over time" or "Just do it," some people would ask, "Yes. But how can I motivate myself to 'just do it'?" The idea of taking action, motivated or not, was new to most people, yet we've all taken out the trash or done our work even when we weren't feeling like it.

When I suggested in one seminar that we have no direct control over, and therefore no responsibility for, the random thoughts that arise, a participant raised his hand and said, "Dan, I just completed an extended yoga certification program that encourages us to practice positive thinking."

I agreed that it was more pleasant to have positive thoughts than negative ones, and that I would cultivate this capacity if it were under my conscious control. "Unfortunately," I said, "no one has a spam filter in their head, nor do we say to ourselves, *I think I'll think this thought next.* Thoughts happen to us, arising in our field of awareness. Sometimes they're positive, sometimes negative."

When I asked the attendees to raise their hand if they'd ever read a book on positive thinking, many hands went up. "Great," I said. "Now keep your hands high if, having read that book, you've only had positive thoughts for, say, the past week or two." Every hand went down. "Ah," I said, "if only you'd read the book twice, and done all the exercises, and used a highlighter…" Then I added: "Or maybe the notion of eliminating negative thoughts is simply unrealistic. Well, it's also unrealistic to assume too much responsibility for arising thoughts and feelings, and not take enough responsibility for behavior."

I realized in that moment that I was sounding a lot like the Sage. It always took me time to shift from role-modeling (imitating others) to finding my own way of expressing what I'd understood and embodied.

Then another question broke into my introspective moment: "What about anger management courses?" someone asked.

"Anger management courses don't really manage anger; they manage behavior. And while our emotions, beliefs, and circumstances all create *tendencies* to behave a certain way, we're here to rise above those tendencies. We do all the time — when's the last time you went to school or work or made progress on a task even though you weren't in the mood?"

I recalled the exemplary life of my friend and gymnastics teammate Rick Field, who, according to Coach Frey, was "the only gymnast I've ever coached who *never* had a bad workout." In middle school, Rick was, in his own words, "overweight, unathletic, and getting mostly C grades." But when he entered high school, after being teased for years by an insensitive stepfather, "something snapped," as Rick told me. "I made a vow that from then on, I'd earn straight A's through high school and college and become a top gymnast."

Rick reorganized his life and priorities to make good on his vows. What he lacked in talent he made up for with discipline. And in the gym he never broke form. Earning straight A's, he went on to a PhD in physics, wrote five papers with his friend and colleague Richard Feynman, and spent years teaching theoretical physics. (Rick Field also had a sister named Sally, who did quite well in the acting field.)

I was inspired by other teammates too, like Eric Courchesne, who first walked into the gym supported by crutches and leg braces due to childhood polio; he went on to win a conference championship on the still rings. And Tom Bruce, who trained on every event despite being legally blind.

My early life and role models like Rick and Eric and Tom prepared me for a constructive life long before I met the four mentors. I knew even then that actions mattered more than words. Or, to paraphrase E. M. Forster, "How do I know what I think until I see what I do?"

Another Take on Enlightenment

A central theme of some spiritual traditions is the ascension of consciousness up through the chakras into higher realms. In fact,

I'd once envisioned awakening as a dramatic event with ecstatic visions and feelings of bliss, peace, harmony, and happiness. Now I lived more in accord with this definition of Zen: "When I'm hungry, I eat. When I'm thirsty, I drink. When I'm tired, I rest" — flowing with the Tao, or natural way, relating to each moment as it comes, without added complications.

In this light, the Sage's Six Stair Steps to Enlightenment provided a sharp contrast to the Professor's levels of consciousness or the Guru's seven stages of life. My notes summarized his stair steps as follows:

Step One: I'm upset and don't even notice that my room is a mess.

Step Two: I'm upset, but I notice that my room is a mess, and it bothers me even more to live in a messy room. But I do nothing about it.

Step Three: I'm upset, but I notice that my room is a mess and begin to clean it to try and reduce my upset feelings.

Step Four: I'm upset and, noticing my messy room, I clean up because the room was messy and needs cleaning — a shift from feeling-centered to purpose-centered behavior. I still believe that the room gets cleaned solely through my own efforts.

Step Five: Still upset, I notice and clean my messy room, thanks to a parent who taught me to vacuum, to the inventor of the vacuum, and to the people who provide the electricity. No longer a lone heroic figure creating my life, I'm part of a team of countless people. I realize there are no self-made successes.

Step Six: I may still be troubled by anger, sorrow, fear; that is, my emotions haven't necessarily changed. But when I notice my room is messy, I view myself as reality's way of getting work done. Thanks to the support of many people, cleaning is happening. (Now we're in Zen territory.)

The Sage reminded me that no one attains the final step on a permanent basis. In reality, we move up and down the steps, moment to moment.

My notes from the training also contain a thought-provoking CL koan: "Would you rather live with a Buddha who acted crazy, or live with a crazy person who behaved like a Buddha?" In other words, which matters more: someone's inner life, or the behavior they bring into the world? That koan didn't require an answer, but it was a useful question to ponder.

New Insights, New Behavior

Each of my books served as a marker of my spiritual evolution and career path. In the winter of 1996, insights I'd gleaned from the Sage helped shape several sections about the twelve arenas of personal growth in a book I'd conceived years before: *Everyday Enlightenment.*

By this point, due to the Sage's reminders, I no longer encouraged anyone to feel happy or grateful, loving or peaceful, courageous or confident or kind. Instead, I encouraged them to *behave* that way. This advice struck some people as inauthentic, like pretending to be serene when feeling angry. Others mistook my words for the old "Fake it 'til you make it" meme. But it had nothing to do with faking a feeling or trying to generate those feelings. It had to do with taking action.

To clarify this new approach, I've asked: "What if you were afraid of running into a burning house to save a child but you did it anyway — feeling terrified while behaving courageously?"

(Boxing coach Cus D'Amato put it this way: "Heroes and cowards feel the same fear — they just respond differently.")

The example of feeling afraid but acting bravely also applies to any other emotion and behavior, such as feeling shy but acting with confidence, or feeling irritated but showing courtesy. It's an acquired skill, to be sure, but like any other skill it improves with practice.

A Series of Moments

In my teachings I pointed out, as the Sage had before me, that life is composed of a series of moments. Each of us has stable and neurotic moments, intelligent and ignorant moments, irrational and enlightened moments. So when someone approached me after a seminar and said, "Dan, I feel so inspired," I could only respond, "Don't worry, it'll pass."

Since inspiration passes, and motivation comes and goes, I stopped seeking or relying on either one when it was time to write or exercise or do whatever else I needed to do. That's why I recommend to others what I do myself: Choose a goal, and then apply effort over time. Dream big, but start small; then connect the dots.

After a talk, when I was signing books, an attendee said to me, "You seem like a really nice guy, Dan."

"Sometimes," I replied.

A Lofty, Challenging Path

Almost as soon as I began integrating "reality's reminders" into my own work, I discovered the challenges of sharing CL perspectives with attendees accustomed to supportive, inspirational, motivational messages. After spending several years riding the waves of the Warrior-Priest's dramatic appeal to the Basic Self, I now realized that few people were willing to contemplate their debt to countless other people or functioning well no matter what they were feeling. Which is perhaps why many responded to these reminders like taking a bitter medicine they grudgingly knew was good for them.

The challenges of teaching (and living) CL principles did not mean the Sage was wrong. (How can reality be wrong?) Along with the teacher Byron Katie, the Sage is one of reality's greatest advocates and devotees. However, Katie gave suffering people four questions to rely upon — a technique they could apply to stop resisting and start embracing reality. (And people do love techniques and processes that help them feel better.)

I'm still not certain whether CL teachings change people's behavior or, instead, selectively attract altruists who already thrive on critical self-examination. I've found that few people (including me) can consistently meet the Sage's lofty standards. For example, while many other teachers recommend taking regular walks, the Sage takes it to another level, encouraging walkers to bring along a garbage bag and pick up litter along the way.

Some critics of the Sage's work propose that it's better suited to the Japanese culture. The Sage typically replies, "Sony, Toyota, and Mitsubishi products work quite well elsewhere." True enough, but a Toyota isn't a teaching. *Naikan* reflection may work best for those who resonate with Japanese culture and temperament. (At CL instructor gatherings, I noted, people's behavior and manners began to resemble those of traditional Japanese, stopping just short of bowing to one another.)

When I first met the Sage, I was an established teacher seeking fresh perspectives to help refine my work. I approached his CL teachings as with my previous mentors, taking a deep dive to find my way inside the knowledge, a new way to look at reality and the world.

Since then I've taken a step back. Realizing that few people (including my workshop participants) are ready for CL teachings,

I've returned once again to the peaceful warrior's way. I've approached new learning as each of my mentors had done — taking essential elements I'd learned and embodied, then expressing them in my own way, through my words and through my life. This is all any teacher can do.

I retain an abiding appreciation for David Reynolds and his work, and we've maintained a collegial relationship based on mutual respect.

Lives and Deaths of the Four Mentors

The time had come to put the past behind me and to speak with my own authority, while holding a special place in my memory for each of the mentors I've introduced in this book.

The Professor's unrivaled spiritual curriculum and practice, designed to generate self-knowledge to the point of illumination, integrated attention and physical vitality through breath and movement. The Guru's transcendent teaching offered a relationship rarely encountered (or desired) by most independent Westerners, demanding everything and returning, as *prasad* or grace, an enlightened way of living. The Warrior-Priest befriended me, offering validation in a time of need, opening new vistas I could share with others. The Sage's down-to-earth teachings helped reconnect me with the simple reality that life boils down to what we do, moment to moment, with the support of countless others.

Today I recall my mentors not as Professor, Guru, Warrior-Priest, and Sage, but as Oscar, Franklin, Michael, and David — human beings whose combination of gifts, desires, and experiences steered them into lives as unexpected as yours or mine.

As I write this memoir, the Sage is alive and well, in his early eighties, living with his wife on the Oregon coast. My other three mentors have passed into memory.

The Professor, Oscar Ichazo, spent his elder years on the Hawaiian island of Maui until his death of natural causes in 2020 at the age of eighty-nine. Some of his voluminous writings may one day be published. For now, the Arica School and the curriculum he bequeathed to humanity still burn like embers beneath the snow, abiding as his legacy.

The Guru, known as Adi Da in the final decades of his life, after living in seclusion at his Fijian sanctuary and creating visual art, died in 2008 at the age of sixty-nine of cardiac arrest. Despite a comment he'd made years earlier that "dead gurus can't kick ass," a handful of his remaining followers, most living in Fiji, testify that they feel his presence more than ever. Some former students, now older and wiser, are glad to put that era behind them, but a small group remain devoted to his memory, and all of us carry a measure of the light and the shadow that he was.

Michael Bookbinder, the Warrior-Priest, returned to his beloved Alyeska, Alaska, where he renamed himself Snow Leopard. In a sad irony, this once-dashing teacher who'd rescued people from cults apparently created a cult of his own, whose members referred to him by romanticized terms such as Reverend, Commander, and Miquon Medicine Chief. He died from a stroke in 1999 at fifty-five years of age after an active and dramatic life of service that touched many lives.

I measure my mentors not by how they died but by how they lived, not only by any shortcomings but by their significant contributions.

A Dialogue with Socrates

Walking alone in the park, in an expansive moment, I spoke to myself aloud: "Oh, god it feels so peaceful not to be seeking anymore —"

Are you kidding me? said a familiar voice.

"Uh, why would I kid you?"

Then you're kidding yourself, Junior. Of course you're still seeking something. If you weren't, you might as well lie down for good and feed the daisies. Wanting something is what creates interesting literature and lives. Maybe you're not seeking Nirvana, and maybe you have nothing left to prove. But aren't you still seeking to help others, to share new perspectives?

"Well, sure, but I don't feel driven in the same way. Not like I used to — I'm content just to live constructively —"

Now you're sounding like that David Reynolds fellow, who, by the way, has a low bullshit rating in my view.

"I agree. That's why he appealed to me after the heavy hitters like the Professor and the Guru, and then the dramatics of the Warrior-Priest. Anyway, like I said, I'm satisfied just to be here on earth, where I am, as you've reminded me —"

As you already understood, Dan, or you couldn't have written it.

"But maybe I didn't know it *until* I wrote it."

I can't say — I'm not the writer.

"But you're the muse who inspired it all, Socrates!"

Nice to be appreciated. Even if I don't really exist.

"An arguable point."

So what does seventy-five-year-old Dan Millman have to say about this fourth mentor and his down-to-earth, ordinary teachings about reality?

"Hmm, well, you remember how Peter Pan returned to Wendy's house to find his shadow? With the Sage's help, I've found my own."

Did you try to stick it back on with a bar of soap? (Apparently he knew his Pan lore.)

"Very funny, Soc. Anyway, in most ways I found David Reynolds down-to-earth. But he's also idealistic, with standards up in the clouds. There's no way I'm going to carry a trash bag and pick up litter because 'litter deserves to be picked up' or because 'cleaning up needs doing.'"

Speaking of quirks, I notice one of yours —

"Only one? That's good news!"

Notice the way you find a mentor, dive in, but later find flaws?

"I didn't know you were also a psychoanalyst."

Jung and I were close. Freud, not so much.

"So what's wrong with moving deeply into a teaching and then moving on? Am I obliged to stay with one teacher forever?"

Just something to notice —

"Speaking of noticing — while I've got you on the line so to speak — you know how mindfulness has become a *thing*? So many books and courses about it! Seems to me that mindfulness boils down to paying attention to what's happening in the present moment, just as it is. I mean, what more is there to say? Oh — except that attending to arising thoughts and feelings is mindfulness meditation, but it seems even more important to be mindful of what's going on around us — noticing the frame, as the Sage pointed out."

You're preachin' to the choir, Junior.

"Anyway, back to my spiritual promiscuity: I hope my readers and students will do the same with me — enjoy my work, then move on. I'm only a bridge to cross on their own path."

Admirable.

"Don't patronize me."

I mean it. Why do you think I've stayed with you all these years?

"Um, is this a hugging moment?"

Hardly.

"Well, while I'm putting it all out there, it seems to me that most people are searching for ways to help them feel good more of the time and feel bad less of the time. They want to feel inspired.

When people tell me that they've read *Way of the Peaceful Warrior* multiple times, I'm tempted to suggest that they might be better off reading more of my books once."

So many books, so little time.

"Which brings me back to that fundamental notion that there is no best teacher, religion, book, path, diet, or anything else — only the best for each of us at a given time of our life."

Respecting people's process — a good place to end, I heard him say before he vanished from my mind, returning to his residence in my heart.

Part Three

TEACHING AND LEARNING IN THE NEW MILLENNIUM

Who dares to teach
must never cease to learn.

JOHN COTTON DANA

My work has evolved over the years. So have I. By the year 2000, and in the decades that have followed, my approach to teaching has changed with the times. What has remained constant are the laws and principles on which the work is founded. As a teacher, I continue to refine my empathic and communication skills. As a student, I strive to retain beginner's mind, open to new lessons in the service of others.

Recent years have brought more learning experiences, both humbling and humorous, straight from daily life.

Chapter 13

Lightbulb Moments

As part of my ongoing search for practical wisdom, I attended a series of evening talks by Zen teacher Reb Anderson, abbot of the San Francisco Zen Center, ordained by Shunryu Suzuki. After the roshi instructed our small group in the basics of zazen, he made a striking comment that proper meditation has two requirements: "First," he said, "you need a stable posture, and, second, you need to die." He meant, of course, to die psychologically, to truly let go of distractions and attachments in order to transcend the mind and the world.

His observation, and the clarity and quiet authority with which he spoke, made another lasting impression on me. Two decades later, the roshi's provocative statement expanded into an element of my novel *The Hidden School*, and would then prompt me to create and teach a meditation on the process of dying — a rehearsal for relinquishing time, objects, relationships, and all the senses, one by one. This four-minute meditation, which I practiced for more than a year before teaching it, has led me to a deeper appreciation for the gift of life.

No Excuses

Based on the proverb "I hear and I forget, I see and I remember, I do and I understand," my workshops have challenged participants to overcome self-doubt and transcend assumed limitations. For example, in 2004, at a retreat center just outside Austin, Texas, our Sunday morning was dedicated to awaking the warrior spirit. One of the exercises involved breaking inch-thick pine boards with a karate-style strike.

Having demonstrated this breakthrough exercise numerous times — from a lunge position, slamming the edge of my hand through the board — I fully grasped the mental, emotional, and physical resources required, the clear intent, focus, and power. Each person had to think *through* the board, not merely to it. "Life develops what it demands," I reminded participants. "You'll each need to apply proper technique and a strong spirit."

I was responsible for teaching the technique; they were each responsible for the spirit they brought to the task. As soon as each person knelt and looked down at the board, I could tell who would accomplish the break. (Those who failed to break the board returned to the line and were given one more chance. If they failed their second attempt, I handed them a hammer to get the job done — technically a fail but still satisfying.)

The first volunteers were usually males with greater size and confidence, some with karate experience. But this time, a diminutive woman named Maggie Newman came forward and told me three things: First, she'd never broken a board; second, her dominant right hand was injured so she'd have to use her left hand; and, third, it was her seventy-ninth birthday. With the eyes and spirit of a tiger, Maggie broke through the board without hesitation. After that, no one in the room had any excuse. I later learned that

Maggie, a senior student of tai chi master Cheng Man-Ch'ing, was a longtime tai chi ch'uan teacher in New York City.

Awakening the Warrior Spirit

Another significant learning opportunity appeared in the person of Matt Thomas, one of my former Stanford gymnastics students. During and after his undergraduate premed and psychology studies, Matt had earned multiple black belts and later created a real-world self-defense technology he called Model Mugging — exactly what I'd sought during my youth. I completed several trainings under his watchful eye.

In early 2000, Matt's system was adapted and refined by Bill Kipp, former US Marine special ops team leader, who created FAST Defense (Fear Adrenal Stress Training). Bill added classes in awareness enhancement, avoidance and evasive techniques, boundary setting, and verbal defense and empowerment drills. After completing Bill's FAST Defense Instructor course, I was trained well enough to at least improve my odds against a single unarmed or armed attacker as well as multiple unarmed assailants.

In 2005 and 2006 I also trained with Vladimir Vasiliev, founder of a school near Toronto, Canada, in the Russian martial art of Systema. This healthful and effective combat-movement system, which evolved over centuries, has no colored belt rankings, no special uniforms, no rigid techniques or rehearsed attacks. Instead, it refines the student's instinctive responses to neutralize an attacker — like learning a new language of movement. I joined a Systema group in Moscow, where we trained at a Special Forces (*Spetsnaz*) base and completed a Thunderstorm obstacle course. Later, some of us visited the monastery island of

Valaam in Lake Ladoga near Saint Petersburg, which became a key site in my novel *The Journeys of Socrates.*

These late-life warrior-spirit trainings brought a sense of peace and security long after the bullies had faded from my life.

A Small Gesture Makes a Difference

While writing *The Journeys of Socrates,* I felt an impulse to contact my former English teacher Mr. Thompson, whom I hadn't seen in forty years. My old high school in Los Angeles no longer had any record, since Mr. Thompson had retired many years before. But the urge persisted, so I called the Board of Education and explained that I wanted to contact a former teacher I'd admired.

When the clerk, who had many Thompsons listed, asked his first name, I said, "Um...*Mister*?" Then it came to me: "His first name was Cochran. Yes, Cochran Thompson." I could still picture his warm smile marked with a scar from a childhood cleft lip surgery.

"I found his information," the clerk replied, "but I don't know if it's current. In any case, I'm not permitted to give out personal information, but you can send a letter to our office, and we'll do our best to forward it."

It was a long shot, but all I could do. So I wrote Mr. Thompson a letter expressing my gratitude to him for his wit, enthusiasm, and encouragement, which had in part led me to a writing and speaking career — describing how he'd reawakened in me a love of reading and writing, and how he must have done the same for countless students in his many years of teaching. I sealed the letter, which I knew might never reach him, if indeed he was even still alive, and returned to my writing.

About three weeks later I received a letter in reply — not from

Mr. Thompson, but from his daughter Mary, who wrote to let me know that my old teacher, then in hospice care, had shed tears when he read my letter, two days before he died. A week later, she read my letter, along with Mr. Thompson's favorite passage from Shakespeare, at his memorial service.

Chapter 14

The Path Goes On

I think of life as a good book.
The further you get into it,
the more it begins to make sense.

HAROLD KUSHNER

Early one morning in May 2006, as part of my weekly work-out routine, I rode my bike up two steep streets in short but intensive bursts of exertion. The climb was tough, the descent exhilarating. At the bottom, due to my speed, I made my customary wide turn — then I crashed.

That same evening, using crutches, I attended the Berkeley premiere of the *Peaceful Warrior* movie, where I'd been asked to speak briefly after the film. As the applause ended and the house lights came on, I crutched slowly down the aisle to the front of the theater. The pressure bandage on my ankle was concealed by my jeans, so a few audience members chuckled, assuming I was joking around since my character in the film spent time on crutches as well.

Then the laughter faded as I explained what had happened

that morning, exactly forty years after the motorcycle crash depicted in the film: "This morning, while racing my bicycle down a steep hill, a gardening truck appeared at the bottom, directly in my path. Rather than collide, I laid the bicycle down — a maneuver that broke my ankle in three places.

"Apparently," I added, "lessons repeat themselves until we learn them. I finally learned that I'm not twenty-five anymore, and that it's time to dial back the high-risk behavior that once served me well on the trampoline." I think the audience appreciated that I'd shown up at all, but I wouldn't have missed it. That theater was just a few blocks from the site of the service station of my youth.

Even as I taught the peaceful warrior's way, the way was teaching me.

Continuing Education

My teaching work continued, not without its humorous and humbling moments: In 2008, still riding a wave of popularity after the *Peaceful Warrior* movie release, I taught a weekend workshop for about a hundred attendees. In the warm afterglow of our weekend together, I offered a few closing words as the site host arrived to share some administrative remarks. Already packed and poised for the drive home, I ended with a brief story about "practicing each moment mindfully," then said my farewells.

As the audience applauded and my host sat down to speak, I headed for the door. Someone called to me: "Hey, Dan, you're still wearing your wireless microphone!" With a sheepish grin, I walked back and handed the microphone to our host and again headed for the door. Delighted by my disorientation, several people yelled, "Dan, your notebook!" Oops. I turned and grabbed it where I'd left it, by the door. Then I waved and departed.

Approaching my car, I realized that I'd left my windbreaker and car keys on the back of the chair now occupied by the administrator. Since I didn't want to interrupt him or disrupt the group, I asked one of the participants who happened to be outside the room if he'd quietly enter and get the items and bring them out to me. I heard roars of laughter from the group inside as they realized that he was fetching yet more items I'd forgotten in my haste to "mindfully" make my exit.

Foundations of the Way

This true story has described aspects of what I've learned over the years from the four mentors and from other life experiences. So what has it all added up to? What principles and practices do I teach today?

My formal teaching work, launched in the mid-1980s, remained something of a patchwork quilt in those early days, still reflecting my mentors' contributions and communication styles. Sometimes I sounded like the Professor; other times, like the Guru or Warrior-Priest or Sage. Imagine a large crystal vat of water with all these sparkling, colorful bits of many teachings — principles, practices, and perspectives — swirling around until, finally, they all settled to the bottom, and I was left with my own clear vision.

My books, meanwhile, found their place in the Self-Help category. Historically, I'm in good company, since the human potential movement owes much to ancient self-help teachers like the Taoists Lao-tzu and Chuang Tzu; the doctrines of Confucius; Athenian philosophers Socrates and Plato; the Stoics Epictetus and Marcus Aurelius; Persian poets Rumi, Hafiz, and Gibran; Vedantic sages and Zen roshis; transcendentalists Ralph Waldo Emerson and Henry David Thoreau; and modern teachers emerging today.

Today, I don't primarily aim to motivate or inspire listeners, since such feelings come and go. Instead, I plant seeds that may bear fruit in times of need — offering big-picture reminders and guidance. I strive, above all, for clarity of expression, relatively free of jargon.

When I wrote *Way of the Peaceful Warrior*, it seemed to me that the pot of gold at the end of every rainbow was the promise of happiness. Since that time I've come to believe that what we most desire is a sense of worth and meaning, connection and purpose.

That sense of purpose, which I found as a young athlete, then lost, and then found again, commands center stage in my writing. I also speak about how to surf the waves of change, eliminate the negative effects of stress, and live in the present. All that I share has emerged naturally and intuitively from the sum of my experiences.

Joy's Memories

Over the passing years, my relationship with Dan has grown deeper and richer. He was my own mentor, in many ways, and I've also offered guidance to him at times. Today we embrace our differences and live as equals. And we appreciate how our experiences have in some sense enriched the lives of our own family and touched the lives of others. We remain grateful for each day together.

Epilogue

Here and Now

Looking for God, Enlightenment, Reality,
is like seeking a path in a field of snow.
If there is no path and you are looking for one,
walk across it. And there is your path.

THOMAS MERTON

I've never considered myself a spiritual teacher, though some people regard me as such. But if spirituality is that which addresses life's higher promise and points to transcendent possibilities, I accept this designation. But since the days of my youth, I've connected to spirit through the body. Having set aside techniques and methods, I now live in a direct relationship with each arising moment.

In my experience, meditation and insight work along with breathing practices and dietary refinements contribute to a holistic perspective that generates resilience in the face of adversity. Knowing and occasionally transcending my tendencies has opened the way to a more relaxed, lighthearted view of myself and the world and its ever-changing dramas.

Today, Joy and I live in Brooklyn, New York, within walking distance of two of my daughters, their husbands, and three of our five grandchildren. Within the fold of my personal and extended spiritual family of students and friends, I'll continue to teach where I'm invited, to learn while I'm able, and to serve while I live.

Nature remains my wisest teacher, revealing her abundant secrets, even this morning as I strolled down a path in Brooklyn's Prospect Park. Glancing up at bright yellow leaves glowing in the morning sun, I caught sight of a gossamer-winged mayfly, whose life is measured not in months or weeks, but in the hours of a single day, reminding me of life's ephemeral nature.

Now well past middle age, I have more years to look back on than forward to, which brings to mind my mortality and, in turn, gives meaning to the life I've been given.

Heading home, the thought arose: *Socrates still lives within me, his voice my own, showing me the way.* Through my muse and my mentors, for whom I retain an abiding sense of gratitude, I've found a way to live with my head in the clouds and my feet on the ground — with a peaceful heart and a warrior's spirit.

Bonus Content

For more info about the four mentors, including their photos and core books, plus photos and videos from my life, go to:

www.peacefulwarrior.com/fourmentors

Acknowledgments

I owe a debt of gratitude to the following people:

My wife Joy read and commented on every draft, from the first overwritten five-hundred-page version through the ninth draft — a monumental task. I'm a better writer (and person) due to her influence.

My daughter Sierra Prasada, a writer, voice actor, and editor, read several drafts. Her astute eye and discernment helped me find the heart of my story.

My longtime freelance editor, Nancy Carleton, offered timely guidance early on as well as a detailed copyedit in the book's final stages.

Early readers Martin Adams, Diane Millman (my sister), David Moyer, Sandra Sedgbeer, and Beth Wilson each offered their unique and helpful points of view.

My old friend and teammate Herb Solomon reviewed selected material about Oscar Ichazo (the Professor), offering clarifications and suggestions.

Author and literary agent Stephen Hanselman of LevelFiveMedia read a later draft and offered useful notes on how I might enhance the work.

My editors at New World Library, Jason Gardner and Kristen Cashman, with the specialized help of cover artists at theBook-Designers and type designer Tona Pearce Myers, transformed a digital manuscript into a work of art in the form of a published book. I also wish to thank proofreader Judith Riotto and indexer Jess Klaassen-Wright for their excellent contributions to the book and to its readers. Even before the book was published, marketing director and associate publisher Munro Magruder and publicity director Monique Muhlenkamp reached out to inform readers about it.

I also want to thank my daughter Sierra Prasada and Serafim Smigelskiy of HiSierrafim Audio for their excellent full-service production of the audiobook edition of this memoir.

Finally, I've drawn inspiration from the memories of my college teammates at UC Berkeley in ways that stand out more with each passing year: Rick Field, Sid Freudenstein, Herb Solomon, Gary Diamond, Josh Robison, Tom Bruce, Eric Courchesne, Art Lloyd, Chuck Jenner, Bill Fujimoto, Pat Bailey, Dennis Rowe, Joel Tepp, Paul Benya, Jim Lindstrom, Phil Rockwell, Judd Hammon, Scott Swanton, Lonnie Kapp, John Ford, Paul Orrechia, Paul Newman, Crodd Chin, Steve Zahm, Ray Hadley, Mac Sutherland, Tom Fashinell; and from the team I later coached at Stanford, including Steve Hug, Bob Anderson, Hector Neff, Ted Miyamoto, George May, Howard Bessen, Leo Holberg, Bob Horowitz, Brian Morgan, Murray Kephart, John White, Shawn Skerrett, and, on the early team, Steve Rochelle, Dan Young, Chris Harrold, Steve Bryson, and Richard Jerome. All of them, while varying in their skill levels, were young men of strong character, who went on to make significant contributions in their respective postgraduate fields.

While the following few people aren't mentioned in this book, it seems right to acknowledge them here: As a college freshman,

I was befriended by Betty and Austin Edwards, who opened their home, hearts, and pantry. Years later, during my early months with the Guru, exercise pioneer Arden Zinn hired me to coach a spirited girls gymnastics team in Atlanta, Georgia, for nine months before Joy and I returned to the San Francisco Bay Area.

My life has also been enriched by a myriad of role models, including my father and mother, childhood friends, martial arts teachers, coaches, teammates, students, and others I've met along the way. While my four primary mentors happened to be male, I introduced two wise women as central characters in *Sacred Journey of the Peaceful Warrior* and *The Laws of Spirit*. I'm grateful for the women, actual and fictional, in my life — most vividly, my daughters Holly, Sierra, and China, and my wife Joy, who has from the beginning served as my muse, role model, North Star, and true compass.

I began writing this book in the early months of the worldwide Covid-19 pandemic. So I'd like to also acknowledge the healthcare professionals, public servants, teachers, and other essential workers who stayed at their posts to keep our societies functioning. And as we look toward the future, may this period of adversity bestow resilience, perspective, and appreciation; may we plant trees whose fruit we will never taste but may sweeten the lives of generations to follow.

Index